PREACH FOR A YEAR #1

Books by Roger Campbell

Preach For a Year # 1
Preach for a Year # 2
Preach for a Year # 3
You Can Win!

PREACH
FOR A
YEAR #1

104 Sermon Outlines
Two complete outlines for every Sunday of the year

Roger Campbell

kregel
PUBLICATIONS

Grand Rapids, MI 49501

Preach for a Year #1, by Roger F. Campbell. © 1988 by Kregel Publications, a division of Kregel, Inc., P.O. Box 2607, Grand Rapids, MI 49501. All rights reserved.

Cover design: Don Ellens

Library of Congress Cataloging-in-Publication Data

Campbell, Roger F., 1930–

Preach for a year #1 / by Roger F. Campbell.
     p.   cm.
   Includes index.
   1. Sermons—Outlines, syllabi, etc. I. Title.
BV4223.C33   1988   251'.02—dc20   87-29400
                                                                CIP

ISBN 0-8254-2329-5 (pbk., vol. 1)
ISBN 0-8254-2330-9 (pbk., vol. 2)

5 6 7 8 Printing / Year 98 97 96 95

Printed in the United States of America

Dedicated to:

Pastor Martin Blok
who first gave me
the opportunity to
preach the Gospel

CONTENTS

INTRODUCTION

A pastor with whom I had shared a sermon outline called to tell me that this practical help had allowed him to have extra time to visit families in his community. In addition, the sermon had gone especially well that Sunday morning.

I knew this man to be an earnest student of the Bible and an able preacher. Without my help, he had led his church in good growth. Nevertheless, he felt this outline had enriched his ministry, and he has since used more of them successfully.

Every minister knows that organizing his thoughts can enable him to communicate truth in a way that makes it stick in the minds of his hearers. PREACH FOR A YEAR is intended to help in this important task.

Let no one think that these sermon outlines can do the preacher's work for him. These are but skeletons awaiting flesh and resurrection.

J.W. Mahood, a fervent Methodist minister of the early twentieth century, wrote:

> Very little of the average sermon is remembered by the hearers. But there is a subtle influence, a spiritual atmosphere, that flows from every Spirit-filled preacher, that makes his words prophetic, that lifts whole congregations into higher realms of living, and that leaves in their lives influences that abide through all the cycles of time. Thirty minutes of such preaching is worth a thousand carefully prepared sermons where the Holy Spirit has no place. The greatest heights of truth and inspiration are not reached by analysis or logic, but only when the human spirit is lifted by the divine Spirit into the realm of the infinite, and the heart is thus brought so near to God that it can hear the whispers of heavenly wisdom and love.

I have chosen to use Roman numerals to designate the Introduction, Body and Conclusion of the sermon rather than the main points. This form allows me to move the entire outline ahead one step and causes the subpoints to be designated by Arabic numerals. Since there are usually more subpoints than main points, this way of outlining eliminates the need to make numerous mental transfers from letters to numbers when stating them to the congregation. If the more conventional outline is preferred, it will be easy to make that adjustment.

These sermon outlines have been effective for me when preaching in churches ranging from small rural to large suburban. But this has only been true when they have been bathed in prayer and delivered after earnest preparation of my heart. Apart from these requirements of power, all sermon outlines are of little use.

Waterford, Michigan   Roger Campbell

HAPPY NEW YEAR!

John 3:3; Romans 6:4; Philippians 3:13–14

I. INTRODUCTION
  A. THE GREETING OF THE SEASON
    1. Countless greeting cards sent through the mails
    2. Salutations and celebrations
  B. THE NEW YEAR IS NOT REALLY NEW
    1. While thousands will shout "Happy New Year," they will awaken to the same old burdens as before
    2. Instead of a Happy New Year, for many, it will be a terrible hangover
    3. There is no magic hour at midnight that suddenly ushers in utopia
  C. WHAT MAKES A NEW YEAR HAPPY?

II. BODY
  A. THE NEW BIRTH (John 3:3–5)
    1. Necessity of the new birth
    2. Many have dreamed of the opportunity of starting over again
    3. What the new birth is not:
      a. It is not baptism
      b. It is not reformation
    4. The new birth takes place upon receiving Christ by faith (John 1:12; 3:16)
  B. THE NEW WALK (Romans 6:14)
    1. There is no one more miserable than the believer who doesn't live right
    2. Let us see the contrast between the old walk and the new:
      a. The flesh and the Spirit (Gal. 5:16–23)
      b. The walk before and after for the Ephesian Christians (Eph. 5:1–16)
    3. The difference between day and night (Rom. 13:11–14)
    4. To practice the new walk, you must feed the new man (2 Peter 2:1–3)

      5. To practice the new walk, you must reckon yourself dead with Christ and alive with Him (Rom. 6)

  C. THE NEW GOAL (Philippians 3:13–14)
      1. Paul's past goals
      2. Your past goals
      3. Paul's past sins and failures
      4. Paul's past victories
      5. Paul willing to forget all that may hinder him in his life for Christ
      6. Do you have a new goal since becoming a Christian?
        a. Does that goal have priority in your life?
        b. Are you willing to forget the past in order to reach your goal?

III. CONCLUSION
  A. AWFUL RESULTS OF NEGLECTING THIS TRUTH
      1. No new birth . . . soul lost
      2. No new walk . . . testimony lost
      3. No new goal . . . rewards lost
  B. PRACTICAL RESULTS OF ACTING ON THIS TRUTH
      1. Salvation, separation, dedication
      2. The joy of living in the center of God's will

RESOLUTIONS OF BIBLE CHARACTERS

Ecclesiastes 5:4

I. INTRODUCTION
   A. RESOLUTION TIME AGAIN
   B. RESOLUTIONS ARE LIMITED
      1. Doing better cannot save us
      2. Works do not commend us to God
   C. THE VALUE OF RESOLUTIONS
      1. It is good to set goals for ourselves
      2. Resolutions of Bible characters
      3. Let's examine some Bible resolutions

II. BODY
   A. JACOB'S RESOLUTION TO GIVE HIS TITHE (Gen. 28:22)
      1. Conditions under which the resolution was made
         a. Jacob fleeing from Esau because he has defrauded him
         b. A resolution made when he has little to give
      2. Some thoughts about tithing
         a. Abraham commenced it (Gen. 14:20)
         b. Jacob continued it (Gen. 28:22)
         c. Malachi commanded it (Mal. 3:10)
         d. Jesus commended it (Matt. 23:23)
      3. Does tithing apply to Christians?
         a. It is clear we are to give a portion of our income (1 Cor. 16:2)
         b. Notice that tithing began before the law was given
      4. This is one of the easiest places to let down
      5. It also is one of the most practical areas to prove faith
      6. Note the challenge of Malachi 3:10
      7. See how the Lord rewarded Jacob (Gen. 32:10)
   B. DAVID'S RESOLUTIONS CONCERNING GOD'S WORD (Ps. 119:15–16)
      1. "I will meditate in thy precepts"
         a. The importance of meditating on God's Word
         b. "For as he thinketh in his heart so is he" (Prov. 23:7)

15

  c. Taking God's Word into our minds on a regular basis
 2. "I will delight myself in thy statues"
  a. Not to be drudgery, but daily delight
  b. Like a love letter from the Lord
 3. "I will not forget thy word"
  a. This calls for memorization
  b. Memorization of the Bible is not just for children
  c. Why not begin to memorize verses each week this year?
 4. The value of a resolve to read the Bible through this year
  a. Four chapters daily gets us through the Bible in a year
  b. Reading three chapters on weekdays and five on Sunday will also help us cover the whole Bible

C. DANIEL'S RESOLUTION CONCERNING A CLEAN LIFE (Dan. 1:8)
 1. The testimony of a teenager (15 years old)
  a. His country taken by a foreign power
  b. He had been chosen to study at the palace
 2. Decided in his heart to dare to be different
 3. So easy to just go along with the crowd
 4. The word "defile" means to soil or pollute
 5. Plenty of pollution around today
  a. Plenty of reading material that defiles
  b. Plenty of viewing material that defiles
 6. A decision for holiness of life will go against the flesh
 7. Holy living always pays dividends

III. CONCLUSION
 A. YOUR RESOLUTIONS FOR CHRIST TODAY
 B. THINK OF THE IMPACT THESE COULD MAKE ON THE NEW YEAR

THE JOY OF SALVATION

Psalm 51:12

I. INTRODUCTION
  A. A PSALM OF CONFESSION
    1. Here is an inside view of a man getting right with God
    2. The baring of a man's heart after an encounter with failure
  B. IT IS ALSO A PSALM OF THE KING
    1. David is the leader . . . politically . . . spiritually . . . even musically
    2. It is a psalm with which we can identify, because we also fail
  C. WE SHALL FOCUS ON JUST ONE STATEMENT IN HIS PRAYER

II. BODY
  A. DAVID HAD KNOWN THE JOY OF SALVATION
    1. "Restore" indicates he has possessed it before
    2. A search of the Psalms reveals that truth
      a. Psalm 9:1: "I will praise thee"
      b. Psalm 21:1: "The king shall joy in thy strength"
      c. Psalm 23:5: " . . . my cup runneth over"
      d. Psalm 34:1: "I will bless the Lord at all times"
    3. There is good reason for this joy
      a. The joy of forgiveness
      b. The joy of assurance of heaven
      c. The joy of the presence of the Lord
      d. The joy of finding the answer to life
    4. This joy is available to you through THE GOSPEL
  B. DAVID HAD LOST THE JOY OF HIS SALVATION
    1. "Restore" indicates that he does not have it right now
    2. David has a lot of company
      a. Many are filled with gloom who were once filled with glory
      b. Many are burdened who once were blessed
      c. Many are sour who once were filled with song

        d. Many are pouting who once were praising
     3. David and the story of his sin
        a. The affair with Bathsheba
        b. Sin has robbed David of his joy
        c. The song is gone
     4. Many can remember a better day. Do you?
  C. DAVID LONGED TO HAVE THE JOY OF HIS SALVATION RESTORED
     1. "Restore" was part of his prayer to get back what he had lost
     2. David prays for his joy to come back again
     3. What is the road back?
        a. It is the road of remembering
        b. It is the road of confession
        c. It is the road of faith
     4. Do you long for that joy again?
     5. You can have it

III. CONCLUSION
  A. PSALM 32: ANOTHER VIEW OF THE SAME MAN
  B. "BLESSED IS THE MAN WHOSE TRANSGRESSION IS FORGIVEN"
  C. HAVE YOU BEEN FORGIVEN?
  D. YOUR JOY WILL RETURN AS YOU RETURN TO YOUR LORD CONFESSING YOUR SINS

THE BIBLE IS THE WORD OF GOD

2 Timothy 3:16

I. INTRODUCTION
 A. THE GREATEST QUESTION OF ALL
  1. Is the Bible really the Word of God?
  2. If not, we are wasting our time
  3. If so, nothing else even compares in importance
 B. WE BELIEVE THE BIBLE TO BE THE VERBALLY INSPIRED WORD OF GOD
 C. WHY?

II. BODY
 A. BECAUSE OF ITS UNITY AND PERFECTION
  1. What a great library it is!
   a. Over 40 different authors
   b. Writing over a period of 1600 years
   c. All agreeing on one central theme
  2. Compared to any other literature, it is a giant
   a. The great classics shrink beside it
   b. The books of the cults do not compare to it
  3. No contradictions. It is always right
 B. BECAUSE OF ITS FULFILLED PROPHECY
  1. The many prophecies
   a. The empires of Daniel's prophecy
   b. The return of Israel and subsequent dispersion
  2. Prophecies concerning Christ
   a. His birth (Isa. 7:14)
   b. The place of His birth (Micah 5:2)
   c. His rejection and death (Isa. 53)
  3. Prophecies concerning the last days
   a. The return of the Jews to their homeland (Ezek. 37)
   b. The rise of Russia (Ezek. 38, 39)
 C. BECAUSE OF ITS SCIENTIFIC ACCURACY
  1. The Bible is not primarily a book of science
  2. Yet when it speaks on a scientific fact, it is right
   a. The creation of man (Gen. 1:26–28; 2:7–25)

        b. Life in the blood (Lev. 17:11)
        c. The roundness of the earth (Isa. 40:22)
        d. The earth in space (Job 26:7)
        e. The rotation of the earth (Luke 17:34–36)

  D. BECAUSE ITS ACCURACY IS GUARANTEED BY JESUS CHRIST
     1. "Heaven and earth may pass away but my words shall not pass away" (Matt. 24:35)
     2. "The scripture cannot be broken" (John 10:35)
     3. "The scriptures must be fulfilled" (Mark 14:49)
     4. "The things men disbelieve in the Bible are confirmed by Christ
        a. The creation (Matt. 19:4–6)
        b. Noah (Matt. 24:37–39
        c. Sodom (Luke 17:39)
        d. Jonah (Matt. 12:39–41)

  E. BECAUSE IT WORKS
     1. "Believe on the Lord Jesus Christ and be saved" (Acts 16:31)
     2. A new creature (2 Cor. 5:7)
     3. Profitable for doctrine, reproof, correction, and instruction in righteousness (2 Tim. 3:16, 17)

III. CONCLUSION
  A. LET THE WORD WORK IN YOU
  B. TURN IT LOOSE IN LIFE
  C. RESPOND TO ITS TEACHING

WHAT IF JOHN 3:16 WERE NOT TRUE?

John 3:16

I. INTRODUCTION
  A. WE ARE WALKING ON FAMILIAR GROUND
  1. The most familiar verse in the Bible
  2. Luther called it the little Bible
  3. It is the favorite verse of children . . . and often quoted to dying people
  B. THE SETTING OF THE VERSE
  1. The verse spoken to a good and religious man to explain salvation
  2. It's use to win this ruler of the Jews to Jesus
  C. BUT WHAT IF THIS GREAT VERSE WERE NOT TRUE?

II. BODY
  A. WHAT IF GOD HAD NOT LOVED THE WORLD?
  1. "For God so loved the world"
  2. Without His love there would be no hope at all
    a. A dark planet hurtling through space without hope
    b. Nothing to live for and no purpose for existence
    c. Every death would be the end of personal hope and every grave a place of despair
    d. A world where prayers were but useless cries to the skies
  3. But God does love the world
    a. Everything speaks of His love
    b. Every sunrise . . . every blade of grass . . . every fountain of water . . . every birth . . . the face of every child
  4. The greatest demonstration of His love is the cross
  B. WHAT IF GOD HAD NOT GIVEN HIS SON?
  1. "That He gave His only begotten son"
  2. God's love would be frustrated without the cross
  3. Real love always demands giving
    a. A man marries; then works, provides, cares
    b. A woman marries and gives of herself for her family

21

       c. A man anticipates his death; so he provides with insurance

    4. God has given His Son, . . . and apart from this there would be no salvation

C. WHAT IF GOD'S OFFER OF SALVATION WERE NOT TO THE "WHOSOEVERS"?

    1. "That whosoever"

    2. The wonderful word that is general yet particular

    3. It embraces all and yet touches each one

    4. It reaches out to you

    5. Suppose God had offered salvation only to the rich

    6. Suppose God had offered salvation only to the healthy or educated

    7. But God calls all people, individually to trust Him

D. WHAT IF GOD'S OFFER WERE NOT BASED ON FAITH ALONE?

    1. "Believeth"

    2. Picture men working, trying, dying

    3. Picture men learning, earning, failing

    4. Consider the dying thief . . . and the offer to dying men

III. CONCLUSION

A. BUT JOHN 3:16 IS TRUE!

B. YOU CAN BE SAVED BY FAITH IN CHRIST

C. WHAT A MESSAGE TO TAKE TO THE WORLD!

JOY OVER JUST ONE SAVED

Luke 15:10

I. INTRODUCTION
  A. LOOKING IN ON SACRED SCENES
    1. Christians go to heaven when they die
    2. But what do they do?
    3. How much do they know of earth's happenings?
    4. Here is one thing that brings heaven joy: the salvation of sinners
  B. JOY IN THE PRESENCE OF THE ANGELS OF GOD
    1. Not necessarily by the angels . . . but in their presence
    2. Christians who have gone to heaven rejoice over every earthly conversion
    3. Making heaven's inhabitants happy
  C. WHY?

II. BODY
  A. BECAUSE OF THE IMPORTANCE OF THE SOUL
    1. "What shall it profit a man if he shall gain the whole world and lose his own soul?" (Mark 8:36)
    2. The mad race in this world to possess things
    3. But title deed to the entire earth would not be enough to compensate for the loss of the soul
    4. How much attention we give to the body!
      a. Body-building courses
      b. Dressing up the body, fixing up the body, face lifts
      c. Yet little attention to the soul
    5. The importance of soul-winning
  B. BECAUSE OF THE INCREASE OF HEAVEN'S POPULATION
    1. Every soul won is one more that will be in on the joy there
    2. Joy that is shared is multiplied
    3. The indescribable blessings there . . . the beauties
    4. The fellowship there with saints and with the Lord

C. BECAUSE OF THE INVESTMENT OF THE SAVIOR
1. This is the reason He came to earth
2. He could have called ten thousand angels . . . but He died alone
3. All that is involved in His suffering and death for us
   a. His suffering in Gethsemane
   b. His trial . . . the scourging . . . the crucifixion
   c. The precious blood of Jesus (1 Peter 1:19)
4. The purpose of redemption
D. BECAUSE OF THE REALITY OF HELL
1. Each one saved is another plucked from the burning
2. See Luke 16:19–31: the rich man and Lazarus
3. It is amazing what people will risk for a little money
4. The trade-off doesn't make sense
5. Same thing in the area of pleasure for a season
6. The joy of heaven compared to the awfulness of hell
   a. The forgotten doctrine
   b. Need to move to the brink of hell for a glimpse of motivation

III. CONCLUSION
A. MAKE HEAVEN GLAD
B. REACH OUT TO LOST SINNERS EVERY DAY
C. THE LOST SHEEP
D. JESUS IS STILL SEEKING LOST ONES TODAY

INVENTORY TIME IN THE PIG PEN

I. INTRODUCTION
   A. INVENTORY TIME
      1. That time when a businessman must take time to count all his possessions
      2. The time when the facts must be faced for profit or loss
   B. THE YOUNG MAN WHO TOOK INVENTORY IN A PIG PEN
      1. When all was counted, he found he had great loss
      2. His resolution, "I will arise and go to my father"
   C. WHAT HAD BROUGHT HIM TO SUCH LOSS AND WHAT HE DID ABOUT IT

II. BODY
   A. HE HAD THOUGHT ONLY OF GOODS . . . INSTEAD OF GOD (vv. 11, 12)
      1. Perhaps the tenderest story told by Jesus
         a. The father, a good and compassionate man
         b. The great grief brought to the father
      2. Someday a part of all these things will be mine
         a. Surely no thought of God here
         b. The father approached for the inheritance
      3. He would find those goods empty, but now they seemed important
      4. He is not the only one who has found *things* empty
         a. Solomon's search (Eccl. 1:12—2:11)
         b. The rich young ruler (Luke 18:18–25)
      5. Your life may be saying to the Heavenly Father:
         a. "I want my share of goods"
         b. "I'll neglect the Bible if necessary to get them"
   B. HE THOUGHT ONLY OF HIS FLESH . . . INSTEAD OF HIS FUTURE (vv. 13–16)
      1. "Wasted his substance in riotous living"
      2. Had to get into that far country, away from his father
      3. Thought so many of his problems would be settled by getting away

25

        a. So many today . . . a new environment
        b. Daniel 12:3: "Many shall run to and fro"
    4. The cry of the flesh
        a. Ephesians 2:3; 5:1–8
        b. The cry of the flesh is for feeling
    5. Here now you have the two directions in which men move
        a. Those who are searching for satisfaction in goods
        b. Those who are searching for satisfaction in feelings, drugs, booze or other pleasures
    6. The sad picture in the pigpen

C. HE FACED THE FACTS . . . INSTEAD OF FEIGNING HAPPINESS (v. 17)
    1. "When he came to himself"
    2. "How many hired servants have bread enough and to spare"
    3. He did not ignore the situation as some might have done:
        a. "I'm hungry, but I guess everybody else is too"
        b. "I'm feeding pigs, but lots of others are also"
    4. Some excuse their spiritual misery by thinking everybody is in the same boat
    5. He responded to the truth and it changed his life

III. CONCLUSION
A. THE GREAT RESOLUTION (vv. 18–24)
    1. "I will arise and go to my father"
    2. The father awaits and welcomes him
B. FORGIVENESS AWAITS ALL WHO COME TO GOD THROUGH CHRIST
C. COME HOME TODAY

THE SINS OF THE PRODIGAL'S BROTHER

Luke 15:25–32

I. INTRODUCTION
   A. THE PRODIGAL'S RETURN, THE GLAD SCENE
      1. The father running to meet the prodigal
      2. The joy over the returning one
   B. THE MAN WHO MISSED OUT ON THE BLESSING
      1. The elder brother returns from the field
      2. He refuses to enter into the joy and therefore misses out
      3. What caused the elder brother to miss the joy of this occasion?

II. BODY
   A. THE SIN OF A NEGATIVE, CRITICAL, GRUMBLING SPIRIT (v. 28)
      1. Today, one of the principal evidences of our need is our negativism, our complaining, our griping
      2. How different we are from those early saints
         a. Paul could praise in prison and we pout in prosperity
         b. Paul gloried in his infirmities and we growl in affluence
         c. If you growl all day, don't be surprised if you're dog-tired at night
      3. Never have Christians had so much and appreciated it so little
      4. What some Christians grumble about:
         a. Some grumble about their family members
         b. Some grumble about their jobs, the government
         c. Some even grumble about their Father's weather
         d. Some are specialists at finding faults
         e. Some grumble about their churches, pastors
      5. Revived hearts find enough in Jesus to keep them praising!
   B. THE SIN OF AN OFFENDED SPIRIT (vv. 29, 30)
      1. The problem: "When this thy son was come"

    2. How much of the work of God is hindered by this sin

    3. What an offended spirit did to him:

       a. Made him grumble when it was time to glory (vv. 28, 29)

       b. Made him exaggerate his own righteousness (v. 29)

       c. Made him feel sorry for himself (v. 29)

       d. Made him exaggerate another's sins (v. 30)

       e. Made him forget all he had as a son of the father (v. 31)

    4. No wonder things are not as they ought to be: you've something against another. Make it right!

  C. THE SIN OF A COMPASSIONLESS HEART (v. 30)

    1. Why was the prodigal's brother unmoved by his return?

    2. Because he had been unmoved at his being away

    3. He had worked hard on the family farm but was unlike his father. He didn't care about his missing brother

    4. The Father cares. Do you?

III. CONCLUSION

  A. THE ELDER BROTHER NEGLECTED BECAUSE OUR SINS ARE REVEALED THROUGH STUDYING HIM

  B. DO YOU SEE YOURSELF IN THIS WAYWARD SON?

  C. CONFESS THOSE "RESPECTABLE SINS" AND KNOW THE JOY OF THE LORD AGAIN

WHEN CHRISTIANS SUFFER

1 Peter 4:12−19

I. INTRODUCTION
   A. SUFFERING IS AN UNPOPULAR SUBJECT
      1. Salvation is more pleasant than suffering
      2. Heaven is more pleasant than heartache
   B. BUT SUFFERING IS A REAL PART OF LIFE
      1. Every hospital we pass says that suffering is real
      2. Screaming sirens each night say suffering is real
      3. Not only physical but mental anguish
         a. Ann Landers and her success
         b. Suicide prevention organizations
   C. CHRISTIANS ALSO HAVE TRIALS

II. BODY
   A. IT IS NOT STRANGE THAT CHRISTIANS HAVE TRIALS (v. 12)
      1. Some thought that salvation meant no more trials
      2. But it's not an easy road we are traveling to heaven
      3. Christians have trials because we live in a sinful world
         a. We are part of a fallen race
         b. A world of wars and rumors of wars
         c. A world of tornadoes and earthquakes
         d. A world where sin runs rampant and greed brings violence
      4. Christians have trials because of the power of Satan
         a. We have an adversary (Eph. 6:11−12)
         b. See the very real work of Satan on Job
         c. Don't be surprised when he attacks you
      5. Christians have trials because we are on a collision course with this world
         a. Why Jesus was despised and rejected (John 15)
         b. His life was in opposition to the course of the world
         c. Therefore, through the centuries Christians have suffered

B. BUT THE CHRISTIAN'S TRIALS ARE DIFFERENT (vv. 13, 14)
   1. He does not suffer alone
   2. Other Christians stand with him in suffering
   3. He has the day of glory ahead (Rom. 8:18)
   4. He can find joy even in jeopardy (Acts 16:25)
   5. He can rejoice even in reproaches (Matt. 5:11)
   6. Even in his dark hours, Christ is working in him
C. SOMETIMES CHRISTIANS BRING SUFFERING UPON THEMSELVES (vv. 15–19)
   1. Let none of you suffer as a murderer (1 John 3:15)
   2. A busybody: Someone who murders people's reputations
      a. Some think they are looked down upon for their testimony when it is only for their meanness
      b. Don't invite suffering through hypocrisy
   3. Sometimes Christians engage in habits or practices that bring suffering
   4. Sometimes Christians suffer because of backsliding and the resultant chastening (Heb. 12:6, 7)

III. CONCLUSION
   A. ARE YOU WILLING TO SUFFER AS A CHRISTIAN?
   B. SUFFERING NOW BUT GLORY LATER
   C. MAKE NECESSARY LIFE CHANGES TO AVOID BRINGING SUFFERING UPON YOURSELF

WHAT TO DO WITH LIFE'S CARES!

1 *Peter* 5:7

I. INTRODUCTION
   A. JOSEPH PARKER'S ADVICE TO PREACHERS:
      1. "Preach often to those with troubled hearts"
      2. Taking Parker's advice today
   B. A FAMILIAR BUT NEGLECTED TEXT
      1. Some texts ignored because they are familiar
      2. There is a reason: They are rich
      3. Consider John 3:16, John 14:27, Romans 8:28
   C. A TEXT FOR TROUBLED BELIEVERS

II. BODY
   A. YOU ARE IN THIS VERSE
      1. Casting all *your* care upon Him
      2. So much in this world is impersonal
         a. The age of bigness and numbers
         b. Social Security, insurance policies, credit cards
         c. The national product code, scanners, computers
         d. Foreshadows the day when the Antichrist will assign every person a number and require it for anyone to buy and sell
      3. But God still knows you as an individual
         a. God doesn't keep track of His own by cosmic computers
         b. He knows His own by name (John 10:3)
      4. Jesus and the individual
         a. Zacchaeus and his hiding in the tree (Luke 19:1–10)
         b. The woman who touched the hem of His garment (Matt. 9:20–22)
         c. The children: He laid His hands on them and prayed (Matt. 19:13–15)
         d. Even those who were demon-possessed (Matt. 17:14–18)
      5. God has time for you

31

B. YOUR CARES ARE IN THIS VERSE
  1. Casting all your *care* upon Him
  2. Kinds of cares
     a. Cares about your family, children, wife, husband
     b. Finances, future, job, security, public opinion
     c. Business, a coming depression, debts
     d. Health, health of others, mental health
     e. World conditions, war, nuclear destruction
  3. Every care that you are carrying is in this verse
  4. Cares are roadblocks to blessings
  5. With cares removed we can experience the joy of the Lord
  6. The joy of the Lord is your strength (Neh. 8:10)
C. JESUS IS IN THIS VERSE
  1. Casting all your care upon HIM . . . HE CARETH FOR YOU
  2. No one understands like Jesus
  3. "Does Jesus care when my heart is pained?" He cares!
  4. "Who cares when my heart is weary?" He cares!
  5. He waits to take all your cares

III. CONCLUSION
  A. DO YOU WONDER IF HE CARES???? THEN GO TO THE CROSS
  B. THE ONE WHO CARED ENOUGH TO SAVE US WILL CARE FOR ALL OUR CARES

TRIUMPH IN TROUBLE

Job 19:25

I. INTRODUCTION
   A. JOB REMEMBERED BY MANY DURING TROUBLE
      1. His story
      2. His trouble greater than most
   B. JOB'S THREE QUESTIONS
      1. Who can bring a clean thing out of an unclean (14:4)?
      2. If a man give up the ghost, where is he (14:10)?
      3. If a man die shall he live again (14:14)?
   C. JOB DEFEATING DEPRESSION
      1. His confidence in the living Redeemer
      2. His faith reached beyond his present plight

II. BODY
   A. JOB'S FRIEND (v. 25)
      1. "I know that my redeemer liveth"
      2. The failure of Job's earthly friends
      3. The work of the redeemer (Lev. 25:25–55)
         a. The relative in dire need
         b. The redeemer comes and frees him
      4. Rescue brings responsibility
         a. Deuteronomy 7:8: Love and obey him
         b. Deuteronomy 15:15: Show his love and care to others
         c. Deuteronomy 24:18: Show compassion and mercy
      5. Redemption is reason for praise (Ps. 107:2; 136:24)
   B. JOB'S FAITH (v. 25)
      1. I *know* that my Redeemer liveth
      2. Notice Job's confidence
      3. Job's redeemer identified
         a. Christ is the Redeemer (Gal. 3:13; Rom. 3:24; Col. 1:14; 1 Peter 1:18; Rev. 5:9)
         b. He ever liveth (Heb. 7:25; Rev. 1:17–18)
         c. He will stand in the latter day upon the earth (Rev. 5:10 and 19)

     4. Death all about him, but he knew his Redeemer lived

     5. Children dead and he seemed on the verge of death

     6. Job had a sure hope in a world of uncertainty

  C. JOB'S FUTURE (vv. 25–27)

     1. "In my flesh I shall see God"

     2. His Redeemer and his God are one and the same

     3. "Whom I shall see for myself"

     4. I want to see my Savior first of all

     5. All that is involved in Job's future

       a. The finished work of the Redeemer (Rom. 8)

       b. Job sure of the resurrection

       c. We can be sure also (1 Cor. 15)

III. CONCLUSION

  A. MEET JOB'S FRIEND

  B. EXPERIENCE JOB'S FAITH

  C. SHARE JOB'S FUTURE

WHAT IS THAT TO THEE?

John 21:22

I. INTRODUCTION
   A. EIGHT WORDS THAT CAN CHANGE YOUR LIFE
      1. A question and a command
      2. The question: "WHAT IS THAT TO THEE?"
      3. The command: "FOLLOW THOU ME"
   B. A NEW CHAPTER IN PETER'S LIFE
      1. He had left all to follow Christ
      2. He had denied his Lord three times
      3. After the resurrection: Fishing . . . the setting of this scene:
         a. Questions: "Do you love me more than these?"
         b. The Lord's revelation of Peter's ministry and death
         c. What shall this man do? What is that to thee?

II. BODY
   A. CONSIDER THE LORD'S QUESTION IF YOU ARE ALLOWING ANOTHER PERSON TO KEEP YOU FROM TRUSTING AND SERVING THE LORD
      1. What is that to thee?
      2. Now we are in a sensitive area:
         a. So many look at the failures of others
         b. So many hide behind the hypocrites
      3. Remember: you are not accountable for the sins of others
         a. Every one of us shall give an account of himself (Rom. 14:12)
         b. No excuses when we stand before God
      4. The person closest to you may be keeping you from Christ
         a. Maybe it is the failure of your wife or husband
         b. Maybe it is the failure of your boss or neighbor
      5. Look past the failures of others . . . to Christ
      6. What if others fail? What is that to thee?

B. CONSIDER THE LORD'S QUESTION IF YOU HAVE BEEN HURT BY ANOTHER CHRISTIAN
   1. How cruel some Christians can be!
   2. And how self-righteous they can often seem
      a. Many used to serve fervently who have been hurt by others
      b. The cause of Christ harmed by careless tongues
      c. Bitterness has replaced blessing for many wounded believers
      d. Casualties of caustic remarks and gossip groups are everywhere
   3. See how gossip distorted the situation in this text
   4. Has your Christian life or service been injured by thoughtless ones?
   5. Have others failed you?
   6. What is that to thee?
C. CONSIDER THE LORD'S QUESTION IF YOU ENVY ANOTHER'S TALENTS OR POSITION
   1. "Lord, what shall this man do?"
   2. Peter wants to compare his work to that of John
      a. "I am going to feed the sheep. What will John do?"
      b. "I am going to die as a martyr. What will John do?"
   3. Have you been losing God's best because you are envious?
      a. Another's position? Talents? Speaking ability?
      b. Another's success? Money? Attention?
   4. What is that to thee? Follow thou Me!
   5. God often chooses to use those who think they have little to offer
   6. He often uses those who, others think, have little to offer

III. CONCLUSION
   A. NOW WE HAVE CONSIDERED THIS SENSITIVE AREA OF LIFE
      1. Perhaps the area of failure to you
      2. It is time to face the Lord's question: "WHAT IS THAT TO THEE?"
   B. IT IS TIME TO HEED THE LORD'S COMMAND: "FOLLOW THOU ME!"

WHAT MANNER OF MAN IS THIS?

Mark 4:35–41

I. INTRODUCTION
  A. THE LONG, HARD DAY OF PREACHING
    1. The crowds so great He had to get into a boat
    2. Just out from the land, He taught them (v. 1)
  B. THE CROWD LISTENS
    1. All gathered along the beach
      a. Some sit on the sand as close to the water as possible
      b. Some let the waves creep over their feet to get relief from the heat of the day
      c. Up the beach, some sit on driftwood and remains of boats
    2. They hear about the sower, the lighted candle, and the mustard seed that is like the kingdom of God
  C. FINALLY, JESUS AND THE DISCIPLES ARE ALONE
    1. The adventure begins: the invitation, the storm, the miracle
    2. What manner of man is this?
II. BODY
  A. HE IS A MAN WHO INVITES US TO TRAVEL WITH HIM (vv. 35–36)
    1. "Let us pass over to the other side"
    2. An invitation loaded with promises
      a. The promise of His fellowship on the journey
      b. The promise of His fellowship on the other side
      c. The promise of safe passage to the other side
    3. How like the Christian life this is
      a. Here on this shore we are often weary
      b. Jesus invites us to travel with Him to the other side
      c. Those who accept His invitation will arrive safely
  B. HE IS A MAN WHO IS WITH US IN ALL THE STORMS OF LIFE (v. 37)
    1. "And there arose a great storm of wind"

    2. What a great storm it must have been!
      a. The high wind . . . the rolling thunder . . . lightning
      b. The waves beat into the ship
    3. How powerful and devastating upheavals of nature can be!
      a. It was not always so
      b. The earth suffers from the fall of man
      c. The earth in travail . . . earthquakes, etc. (Rom. 8:22)
    4. There is a lesson here: storms come to disciples
      a. They were traveling with Jesus
      b. They had obeyed Jesus, yet the storm came
      c. And you may be passing through a storm, though His child
    5. Purposes of storms
      a. Jonah's storm . . . to bring him from backsliding
      b. Paul's storm . . . to open new doors of witness
      c. The disciples' storm . . . to test their faith
    6. But Jesus was with them in the storm
  C. HE IS A MAN WHO IS UP TO THE OCCASION (vv. 38–40)
    1. He was asleep, weary
      a. Compare to Isaiah 40:28, "neither is weary"
      b. Jesus was indeed a man (Phil. 2:5–7; Heb. 4:14–16)
    2. He arose: "Peace, be still" THERE WAS A GREAT CALM!
      a. The waves ceased; the sea flattened
      b. The moon broke through the clouds
      c. The only sounds were the slight movement of the boat and the swift beating of the disciples' hearts
    3. "What manner of man is this?"

III. CONCLUSION
  A. JESUS AND TODAY'S STORMS
  B. JESUS CAN CALM YOUR STORM AND GIVE YOU PEACE

PILATE'S QUESTION

Matthew 27:22

I. INTRODUCTION
  A. THE SETTING AND THE SCENE
    1. The upper room, the last passover, the first communion
    2. The garden of Gethsemane, the betrayal, the denial, Judas' death
    3. Christ before Pilate . . . Pilate before Christ
    4. The earthly judge . . . before the Judge of all the earth
  B. PILATE'S PLIGHT
    1. The attitude of his prisoner
    2. The advice of his wife
    3. The anger of the Jews
  C. THE QUESTION THAT IS TEARING PILATE APART

II. BODY
  A. IT IS A PERSONAL QUESTION . . . "I"
    1. This is one decision the proud judge would rather avoid
    2. The pressures and forces that press upon his mind
      a. His notable prisoner
        (1) The contrast of the two prisoners
        (2) Pilate might have been willing to even have Barabbas decide
        (3) Some think only of the desperate needing Christ
      b. His nervous wife
        (1) Her dream and advice to her husband
        (2) Some think only the emotionally disturbed need Christ
      c. His noisy crowd
        (1) The quiet Christ and the contrast
        (2) Let the crowd decide; some still do that
    3. The final decision lay with Pilate; he could not escape
  B. IT IS A QUESTION THAT DEMANDS ACTION . . . "DO"
    1. Pilate and his wash basin
      a. Trying to escape his decision

      b. Pilate's policy of neutrality
- 2. But this is a question on which you must act, you must decide
- 3. Some options:
  - a. You can decide to receive Him or reject Him
  - b. You can decide to obey Him or disobey Him
  - c. You can decide to openly confess Him or deny Him
  - d. You can make Him Lord of your life or slight Him
- 4. What are you going to do?

C. IT IS A QUESTION ABOUT JESUS . . . "JESUS"
- 1. Pilate's other decisions dwarfed by this one
  - a. You have no other decision as important as this one
  - b. All others temporal, this one is eternal
- 2. The question the whole human race must answer
- 3. About Jesus. Not about the church, religious ceremony, or tithing
- 4. Christ the Creator, Savior, JUDGE!
- 5. Choose between Christ and Barabbas today!

III. CONCLUSION

A. WHAT WILL YOU DO THEN WITH JESUS?
- 1. Personal
- 2. Action
- 3. About Jesus

B. THE CALL TO A DECISION, A COMMITMENT

THREE CROSSES ON CALVARY'S HILL

SERIES ON THE CROSS   *Luke* 23:33–43

I. INTRODUCTION
   A. THREE GREAT INCENTIVES TO LIFE FOR CHRIST
      1. The Holiness of our God (Isa. 6)
      2. The return of Christ (1 John 2:28)
      3. The cross: The greatest demonstration of His holiness and love
   B. LET US LOOK TO CALVARY
      1. Jesus dying there with two thieves: One on either side
      2. One dying for sin. One dying in sin. One dying to sin
      3. Two were completely guilty. One completely innocent
      4. Two paying their debt to society. One paying OUR debt of sin

II. BODY
   A. LOOK TO CALVARY AND SEE TWO MEN IN THE SAME CONDEMNATION (vv. 39–40)
      1. The mockery of the first thief
      2. The other thief and his remarkable observations:
         a. States a great spiritual truth
         b. Recognizes his own guilt (v. 41)
      3. The most difficult truth on earth to accept:
         a. That all people are equally guilty before God
         b. How we divide humanity: RACE . . . FACE . . . PLACE . . . But with God . . . just GRACE
      4. There is no difference
         a. The mayor and the meter maid
         b. The star and the street walker
         c. The doctor and the patient
         d. The warden and the criminal
      5. So hard to realize that all are lost
         a. Joseph Parker: "If only I could find a sinner"
         b. Jesus, the friend of sinners
   B. LOOK TO CALVARY AND SEE TWO MEN WHO BOTH ASK JESUS FOR SALVATION (vv. 39, 42)
      1. Both thieves asked Jesus to save them

      a. "If..save thyself and us"

      b. "Lord..remember me"

  2. The first asked to be saved from the situation

  3. Many pray when in trouble, but this kind of prayer does not save

  4. THE DIFFERENCE: The other asked to be saved from his SIN

      a. Here is genuine conviction

      b. Conviction precedes conversion. ALL GUILTY BEFORE GOD

      c. This thief faces the real issues of life:

         (1) He admits his sin and accepts Christ as his Lord

         (2) He anticipates the resurrection of Christ

         (3) He anticipates his own resurrection

         (4) He looks at Jesus in His humiliation and sees a King

C. LOOK TO CALVARY AND SEE JESUS, WHOSE PURPOSE IS SALVATION

  1. AMEN. The thief prayed and Jesus said AMEN to his prayer

  2. JESUS HAD TIME TO WIN ONE MORE SOUL

  3. Questions answered that day:

      a. Can one be saved in his dying hour?

      b. Can one be saved after a life of wickedness?

      c. Can one be saved without baptism or communion?

      d. Can one be sure of heaven after death?

III. CONCLUSION

A. ALL OF HUMANITY IS SEEN AT THE CROSS

B. TWO WAYS! WHICH WILL YOU TAKE?

THEY WATCHED HIM THERE

Series on the Cross   Matthew 27:36

I. INTRODUCTION
   A. STUDIES IN THE PASSION AND POWER OF OUR LORD
      1. The cross through Easter
      2. This intense hour: Christ's last words, last looks
   B. MOVING EVER TOWARD THE CROSS
      1. The Passover, the Lord's Table, betrayal
      2. The mock trial
      3. Pilate: "Behold the man"
      4. Account of the crucifixion (Matt. 27:27–36)
   C. THE SOLDIERS AT THE CROSS

II. BODY
   A. THEY WATCHED COMPLACENTLY IN THE HOUR OF THE CRUCIFIXION
      1. These soldiers had witnessed many crucifixions
         a. Darius crucified two hundred when conquering Babylon
         b. Alexander crucified two thousand when conquering Tyre
         c. A common means of capital punishment for the Romans
      2. To them, just another execution
      3. This may be the reason the cross means so little to many today
         a. They have mutilated the Master before He reaches the cross
         b. They doubt His virgin birth and reject His deity
         c. They do not accept His miracles. Just another man
      4. Who died that day?
         a. The One of whom the prophets had spoken (Isa. 50:6 and Isa. 53)
         b. The One who was miraculously born (Isa. 7:14; Luke 2:1–14)
         c. The One who could open blind eyes and even raise the dead

43

      5. See who is dying there, and you will never get over it

      6. Gypsy Smith: "I have never lost the wonder of it all"

  B. THEY WATCHED CALMLY IN THE HOUR OF THE WORLD'S GREATEST CRISIS

      1. This was the hour of the ages, and they were not moved

      2. When the darkness came and the earth shook, their leader would finally be shaken and exclaim: "Truly this was the Son of God"

      3. They were just observers as the scene unfolded before them

        a. There were the priests who taunted Him

        b. The thieves who cast the same in His teeth

        c. The wandering disciple afar off in tears

        d. The little band of faithful ones near the cross

      4. The forces of heaven and earth stand poised

        a. He could have called ten thousand angels

        b. The earth hovered between destruction and deliverance

      5. This is also an hour of crisis, and many are unmoved

  C. THEY WATCHED CARELESSLY IN THE HOUR OF GOD'S GREATEST EXAMPLE OF CARING

      1. They had gambled with His garments by casting lots

      2. They heard the words from the cross

        a. "Father, forgive them . . ." (Luke 23:34)

        b. "Today, thou shalt be with me . . ." (Luke 23:43)

        c. "Woman, Behold thy son . . ." (John 19:26)

        d. "My God, My God, Why? . . ." (Matt. 27:46)

        e. "I thirst . . ." (John 19:28)

        f. "It is finished . . ." (John 19:30)

        g. "Into Thy hands I commend my spirit" (Luke 23:46)

      3. They saw it all, knew all the facts, but did not respond

      4. Have you responded to God's love?

III. CONCLUSION

  A. WHAT DOES THE DEATH OF CHRIST MEAN TO YOU?

  B. HOW DOES HIS DEATH AFFECT YOUR LIFE?

  C. TRUST THE ONE WHO DIED FOR YOU

FORGIVE THEM

Luke 23:35

I. INTRODUCTION
   A. THE FOCUS ON THE CROSS TO BRING REVIVAL
      1. The New Testament church our example of revival
      2. The cross and resurrection their message
   B. APPROACHING THE CROSS
      1. The trial . . . the scourging . . . the crown of thorns
      2. The crucifixion itself
      3. The first word of Jesus from the cross

II. BODY
   A. A PRAYER . . . "FATHER"
      1. At that desperate time, Jesus prayed
      2. We have become complacent about the seriousness of the hour
         a. The sky is filled with storm clouds
         b. The prophetic program of the ages is unfolding
         c. The nuclear threat twenty-four hours a day
         d. Time is running out
      3. It's time to pray
      4. Prayer is always the foundation of revival
         a. Moody: "Every great work of God can be traced to a kneeling figure"
         b. 2 Chronicles 7:14: A revival text that emphasizes prayer
         c. Calling churches to prayer
   B. A PRAYER FOR FORGIVENESS . . . "forgive . . ."
      1. What a good word it is!
      2. How good that the record can be made clean
      3. This was the message of the New Testament church
      4. Joseph Parker: "I have a wonderful message if only I could find a sinner"
      5. Christ was able to forgive sins, and this amazed His critics
      6. Are you guilty? Here's good news! Jesus forgives

45

C. A PRAYER FOR THE FORGIVENESS OF THOSE WHO
HAD WRONGED HIM . . . "forgive them"
1. "Then . . ." The first and connecting word
2. The greatest roadblock to revival is the lack of forgiveness among the people of God
a. Old grudges . . . nursing old hurts . . . malice
b. The church crippled by petty grievances
3. Barriers between believers
4. But not one has been wronged as Jesus was wronged
5. You can forgive! Will you?

III. CONCLUSION
A. COME TO THE CROSS!
B. THE CALL TO FORGIVENESS
1. Since He forgave, we must forgive
2. We can forgive because we have been forgiven

TODAY IN PARADISE

SERIES ON THE CROSS   *Luke* 23:39–44

I. INTRODUCTION
  A. FATHER FORGIVE THEM
    1. Should make us forgiving . . . forbearing . . . faithful
    2. The word that withheld the wrath of God
  B. THE SECOND WORD FROM THE CROSS
    1. "Today thou shalt be with me in paradise"
    2. A word of personal assurance . . . and challenge

II. BODY
  A. IT IS A WORD OF PARDON
    1. This word spoken to a man fully aware of his sin
    2. Many things we do not know about this thief
      a. Name
      b. Age
      c. Crime
    3. Evidence of God's working in his heart
      a. Aware of God's knowledge of his heart
      b. Has become reverent toward God (v. 40)
      c. Sees himself as guilty (v. 41)
    4. Assurance that sins are forgiven
      a. Prayer answered
      b. Promise of life from the Lord
  B. IT IS A WORD THAT IS PERSONAL
    1. "With me"
    2. The thief cries out for personal salvation
    3. Lord! Remember me!
      a. The prayer of faith: "Lord!"
      b. Never saw a miracle or heard a sermon
      c. Looked at the crucified and called Him Lord
      d. "Remember me." Expects Him to complete His work
    4. J.C. Ryle, "Surely such faith was never since the world began"

  C. A WORD ABOUT PARADISE
     1. "In paradise"
     2. We will be with Jesus in heaven when we die
     3. The promises and problems solved by this statement
        a. Eternity is just a step away
        b. No soul sleep and no unconscious state
        c. Salvation not by works or religious acts. No time for these left
        d. Believers are going to a better place
     4. What heaven should mean to us

III. CONCLUSION
  A. JESUS WINS ONE MORE SOUL TO TAKE TO GLORY AS HE DIES ON THE CROSS
     1. We have our petty excuses for not reaching others
     2. In all the discomfort and agony of the cross, Christ wins one more
  B. DO YOU HAVE THE SURE HOPE OF THE DYING THIEF?
  C. WHICH THIEF ARE YOU?

WOMAN, BEHOLD THY SON

John 19:25

I. INTRODUCTION
   A. THE FIRST THREE WORDS FROM THE CROSS
      1. "Father, forgive them." Expression of forgiveness by the perfect Son
      2. "Today thou shalt be with me in paradise." Expression of assurance by the perfect Savior
      3. "Woman, behold thy son." Expression of affection by the perfect man
   B. G. CAMPBELL MORGAN ON THESE WORDS
      1. The first: His pity for man
      2. The second: His power towards those who believe in Him
      3. The third: His provision for those upon whom His love is set

II. BODY
   A. THIS WORD REMINDS US OF JESUS AND THE FAMILY
      1. In His dying hour, Jesus speaks of motherhood and sonship
      2. The family is instituted of God
         a. Chose to be born into an earthly family
         b. Chose to accept the training and discipline of a home
         c. Taught that marriage is for life
         d. Insisted on the sanctity of the home
         e. Showed His love for children
      3. Christ longs to be the center of every home
      4. "Except the Lord build a house they labor in vain that build it" (Ps. 127:1)
      5. Happy the home where Christ is truly the head
         a. He wants to remove the strife from your home
         b. He wants to plant love in your home
   B. THIS WORD REMINDS US OF JESUS AND THE FAITHFUL FEW
      1. Only a few are there: four women and one man

      2. Matthew 26:56: "All forsook Him and fled"
      3. But John returns . . . love draws him
      4. How few were the faithful . . . but how faithful were the few!
      5. They stood at the cross
         a. It was not an easy place to stand
         b. Mary and the fulfilled prophecy, "A sword shall pierce" (Luke 2:35)
         c. Men are willing to rally to so many banners and causes
         d. Few are willing to stand at the cross
         e. Martyrs of the cross through the ages, both men and women
      6. Most of the work of Christ has been done by the minority
      7. "The harvest truly is plenteous, but the laborers are few" (Matt. 9:37)

C. THIS WORD REMINDS US OF JESUS AND HIS FAITHFULNESS TO US
      1. "Woman, behold thy son!" "Behold thy mother"
      2. Notice that John is to care for Mary
      3. Jesus cares for Mary's needs:
         a. For her emotional needs . . . has her sent away before the darkness
         b. For her spiritual needs . . . He dies for her . . . and you and me
         c. For her temporal needs . . . John will minister to her
      4. John to be a personal representative for Christ
      5. We are also to be ambassadors and represent Christ to others (2 Cor. 5:20)

III. CONCLUSION
    A. WHAT DOES THIS STATEMENT OF THE CROSS SAY TO YOU?
    B. HOW WILL YOU RESPOND?
    C. WILL YOU ALLOW CHRIST TO BE LORD OF YOUR HOME?
    D. WILL YOU BE FAITHFUL TO HIM EVEN IF IT MEANS BEING IN THE MINORITY?

JESUS IDENTIFIED WITH SINNERS

Matthew 27:46

I. INTRODUCTION
  A. THE FIRST THREE WORDS FROM THE CROSS
    1. "Father, forgive them." Shows His pity for men
    2. "Today, thou shalt be with me." Shows His power to save
    3. "Woman, behold thy son." Shows His provision for those He loved
  B. THE DIFFICULT WORD
    1. Luther gives up: "God forsaken of God, who can understand that?"
    2. This is the word that identifies Jesus with sinners

II. BODY
  A. JESUS IDENTIFIES WITH THE SINNER'S DARKNESS (v. 45)
    1. Darkness descends over the entire earth for three hours
      a. Many explanations for this, but this is supernatural
      b. Phlegon—fourth year of the 202nd Olympiad — a darkness over all of Europe
      c. Tertullian records a worldwide darkness which the statesmen of Rome could not explain
      d. Eclipse impossible: The time of the full moon — too long
    2. Pictures for us the supernatural darkness brought by sin
      a. The mind of man is darkened (Rom. 1:21)
      b. The deeds of men apart from God are called the works of darkness (Rom. 13:12–14; Eph. 5:1–11)
      c. Man yields himself to Satan who is called the prince of darkness (Eph. 6:12)
      d. Sin in its end brings eternal darkness (Matt. 8:12; 22:13)
    3. Jesus, the light of the world, dies in darkness to deliver us from darkness (Col. 1:12–14; John 8:12)

B. JESUS IDENTIFIES WITH THE SINNER'S UNCERTAINTY (v. 46)
   1. My God! My God! Why????
   2. Jesus who was always so certain about everything
      a. The experience with the doctors at age 12
      b. At the wedding in Cana and at feeding of 5,000
      c. When the storm was raging on the Sea of Galilee
   3. The lost man lives in a world of uncertainty
      a. Why am I here?
      b. What is life all about?
   4. This uncertainty leads to agony of soul
      a. Isaiah: "The wicked are like the troubled sea" (Isa. 57:20–21)
      b. The spiritual agony of sin: the drunkard, the thief, the liar, the adulteress, the gossip
   5. Do you feel the agony of soul today that comes from sin?
   6. Jesus feels it with you . . . endured your uncertainty
C. JESUS IDENTIFIES WITH THE SINNER'S SEPARATION FROM GOD (v. 46)
   1. "Why hast thou forsaken me?"
   2. Impossible for the Father to look on Him as He took the sinner's place
   3. John R. Rice: "To understand this, you would have to be sinless and go to hell in that state"
   4. Does not say "Father" but takes the place of a lost soul
   5. He was forsaken that you might never be forsaken (Heb. 13:5)

III. CONCLUSION
   A. IT IS NOT NECESSARY FOR YOU TO CONTINUE IN DARKNESS AND UNCERTAINTY
   B. WILL YOU IDENTIFY WITH HIM?
   C. TURN FROM SIN TO CHRIST AND TRUST HIM AS YOUR SAVIOR

THE THIRSTING SAVIOR

John 19:28

I. INTRODUCTION
  A. IS THE MESSAGE OF THE CROSS CURRENT?
    1. What message is there for men of the space age?
    2. Do the words of the Master apply to men of the age of missiles?
    3. Can the events on a hill 2,000 years ago affect us now?
    4. Can the death of one man by crucifixion affect men in an age when thousands can be killed with one bomb?
    5. Does it matter to men who have walked on the moon that the sun was darkened at high noon?
  B. TWO SHORT WORDS SHOW US HOW CURRENT THIS MESSAGE OF THE CROSS IS: "I THIRST"

II. BODY
  A. JESUS SAID, "I THIRST," BECAUSE HE DIED AS A MAN
    1. John's primary purpose was to show Christ's deity, but here he shows His humanity
    2. Came to feel what we feel and to know our needs
      a. Grew (Luke 2:42)
      b. Wearied (John 4:6), compare to Isaiah 40:28–31
      c. Hungered (Matt. 4:2)
      d. Slept (Mark 4:38)
      e. Wept (John 11:35)
      f. Groaned (John 11:33)
    3. The human race had sinned and must die
    4. He had refused the potion prepared to dull the pain (Matt. 27:34)
      a. He must feel all the pain due humanity
      b. Not one nerve can be less sensitive as He dies for man
    5. Men still feel the same pain. suffering, and needs as they have through the centuries
  B. JESUS SAID, "I THIRST," BECAUSE HE EXPERIENCED THE THIRST OF HELL FOR MAN
    1. The awful thirst of hell (Luke 16:19–31)

53

      a. How real physical thirst can be

      b. A mirage on the desert and how it affects people

   2. Those three hours of darkness as Jesus took our place are difficult to comprehend in His agony

   3. There, compressed into those hours was an eternity in hell

   4. Thus the cry, "My God, My God"

   5. This goes beyond physical thirst to the thirst of the soul

   6. In this space age, people still die and go to hell

   7. In this space age, they still have such spiritual thirst that it drives them to drink, drugs, crime

C. JESUS SAID, "I THIRST," BECAUSE HE MUST FULFILL THE SCRIPTURE TO PROVE ITS MESSAGE TO EVERYONE

   1. "That the scripture might be fulfilled" (Ps. 69:21)

   2. At least 333 prophecies of the Old Testament converge in Jesus

   3. And 240 of these were fulfilled by the time of His ascension

   4. The Word of God is so important to the Savior that He will utter every word necessary to fulfill it

   5. Let others deny it; Jesus declares it to be true

   6. The Bible stands

III. CONCLUSION

A. DO YOU STILL WONDER IF HE CARES FOR YOU?

B. THE CALL TO THIRSTY SOULS

"This frail vessel Thou hast made, no hands but Thine can fill
The waters of this world have failed . . . And I am thirsty still"

IT IS FINISHED

I. INTRODUCTION
   A. IT IS ONLY A FEW DAYS FROM PALM SUNDAY TO THE CRUCIFIXION
      1. How fickle the world's praise!
      2. One day you are crowned, the next, crucified
      3. The sound of hosannas had hardly died when they were crying, "Away with Him! Crucify Him!"
   B. THE SEVEN STATEMENTS OF CHRIST FROM THE CROSS
      1. "Father, forgive them . . ."
      2. "Today, thou shalt be with me . . ."
      3. "Woman, Behold thy son . . ."
      4. "My God, My God . . ."
      5. "I thirst . . ."
      6. "It is finished . . ."
      7. "Into Thy hands . . ."
   C. "IT IS FINISHED." THE SIXTH WORD

II. BODY
   A. THE WORD OF COMPLETION
      1. Many leave this world with their tasks uncompleted
         a. The pen drops from the writer's hand
         b. The painter's brush falls before the painting is done
         c. The chisel tumbles from the grip of the sculptor
      2. But Christ is the great finisher
         a. Creation finished (Gen. 2:1)
         b. The new heaven and earth (Rev. 21:6)
         c. Redemption finished (John 19:30)
      3. What Christ completed on the cross
         a. Completed all the requirements of the law (Col. 2:14–17)
         b. Completed all the Old Testament sacrifices (Heb. 10:11–18)
         c. Completed all the suffering required to pay for our sins (1 John 1:7)
      4. Jesus paid it all

B. THE WORD OF CONQUEST
1. With a loud cry (Matt. 27:50, Mark 15:37, Luke 23:46)
2. Not a sigh of defeat, but a cry of victory!
3. Let it be loud enough for the devil to hear!
a. The promise in the Garden of Eden (Gen. 3:15)
b. Satan and all demons were defeated at Calvary (Col. 2:15)
4. The call of the crowd: "Come down from the cross!"
5. Ten thousand angels stand ready for His call
6. But Jesus stayed on the cross, defeating Satan
7. Enough of this defeated Christianity. WE ARE EQUIPPED TO WIN! WE HAVE A VICTORIOUS CHRIST!

C. THE WORD OF COMFORT
1. The debt of sin is really paid
2. This is only one word in the Greek language: "*Tetelestai*"
3. The word for tax receipts (paid in full)
4. How good it feels to have a bill paid!
5. This is the word that assures peace
6. What this must have meant to the dying thief
7. What peace this must have brought to his heart!

III. CONCLUSION
A. CHRIST PAID YOUR DEBT TOO
B. TRUST IN CHRIST AND BE SAVED
C. REST IN HIS FINISHED WORK ON THE CROSS FOR YOU

THE WORD OF ASSURANCE

I. INTRODUCTION
  A. THE SEVENTH WORD FROM THE CROSS
    1. Begins like the first: "Father"
    2. The first on behalf of others
    3. This one a personal word of His own
  B. LESSONS FROM THE LORD'S LAST WORD

II. BODY
  A. WE CAN ALL HAVE A PERSONAL RELATIONSHIP WITH OUR HEAVENLY FATHER
    1. God has created us for fellowship with Himself
    2. That fellowship was broken by the fall of humanity into sin
    3. Christ came to pay our debt of sin to restore us to God
    4. We are more than bodies and minds
    5. We are body, soul, and spirit (2 Thess. 5:23)
      a. By the body, we are world-conscious
      b. By the soul, we are self-conscious
      c. By the spirit, we are God-conscious
    6. But at the fall all became spiritually dead (Gen. 2:17)
    7. Jesus died to restore fellowship with the Father and give us new life through a spiritual rebirth (Eph. 2:1)
  B. WE COME INTO THIS PERSONAL RELATIONSHIP THROUGH CHILDLIKE FAITH
    1. "Father." How simple and childlike that expression is
    2. Through receiving Christ by faith we become the children of God (John 1:12)
    3. This new relationship makes us part of God's family and all believers become our sisters and brothers
    4. The many promises of provision from the heavenly Father become ours
    5. Our heavenly Father is rich and is able to provide all our needs
    6. No religious act can bring about this new relationship, only faith in Christ (Eph. 2:8, 9)

C. WE CAN HAVE ABSOLUTE ASSURANCE ABOUT LIFE AFTER PHYSICAL DEATH
1. "Into thy hands I commend my spirit"
2. Many lessons here:
    a. Jesus was in full command in His last moments
    b. He was in perfect relationship with His Father
    c. He had perfect reliance upon His Father for everything beyond earth
    d. His death was entirely voluntary
    e. He was completely submitted to the Father's will
    f. He triumphed over death
    g. In death he experienced perfect peace
    h. He expressed His human spirit and the possibility of assurance as to its destination
    i. He did not die as a martyr, but as the Savior . . . God's plan
    j. He came to die, not just as a moral example
    k. He was the substitute for sinners and fulfilled His mission as called for by the prophetic Scriptures

III. CONCLUSION
A. COME IN FAITH TO THE ONE WHO DIED FOR YOU
B. BECOME A CHILD OF THE HEAVENLY FATHER AND EXPERIENCE HIS PEACE IN THE MOST TRYING OF LIFE'S SITUATIONS

AFTER THE CROSS

I. INTRODUCTION
   A. THE SETTING AND THE SCENE
      1. The hour the world had awaited
      2. The Father's love as Isaiah 53 is fulfilled
   B. REDEMPTION IS WROUGHT
      1. The seven last words
      2. The song of the saints through eternity (Revelation 5:9, 10)
   C. AFTER THE CROSS

II. BODY
   A. THE RENT VEIL (v. 51)
      1. The story of the veil (Heb. 9:1–15)
         a. The day of atonement once a year
         b. How the priest came into the holiest place
      2. The veil was torn before the earthquake
      3. The veil torn from the top to the bottom
      4. The entrance now through Christ (Heb. 10:19–21)
         a. The priesthood done away (1 Peter 2:9)
         b. The Law now fulfilled (Col. 2:14–17)
   B. THE RESURRECTION OF THE DEAD (vv. 52, 53)
      1. Speaks of victory over the grave
      2. Notice the graves opened three days before the saints arose
      3. Something different about those graves since Christ died
      4. A Christian grave is a place of anticipation
   C. THE REACTION OF THE CENTURION (v. 54)
      1. How fitting that one should be convinced at Christ's death
      2. "Truly this man was the son of God!"
      3. Tradition says he became a preacher and a martyr
   D. THE REVIVAL OF THE CHRISTIANS (vv. 57–61)
      1. Joseph of Arimathea had been a secret disciple (John 19:38)

   2. Nicodemus now goes public in his faith (John 19:39)
   3. Couldn't remain silent after standing at the cross
   4. Jesus had stood still in judgment — they must walk for Him
   5. Jesus had kept silent in judgment — they must talk for Him
   6. Jesus had died — they must live for Him

III. CONCLUSION
   A. WHAT HAS THE CROSS DONE TO YOU?
      1. How can you put off salvation?
      2. How can you be weak in your dedication?
   B. STAND AT THE CROSS TODAY!

PALM SUNDAY'S TEARS

Luke 19:41–44

I. INTRODUCTION
  A. PALM SUNDAY
    1. So called because of the palm branches used
    2. The triumphal entry, Daniel's amazing prophecy, 483 years (Dan. 9:25)
    3. Recorded by all the Gospel writers
  B. THE SETTING AND THE SCENE
    1. About five days before Passover, Jesus and disciples from Bethany
    2. Most important of feasts to begin, 300,000 pilgrims
  C. PAST THE TRIUMPHAL ENTRY TO PALM SUNDAY'S TEARS
    1. Jesus weeping over Jerusalem
    2. The lessons about our Lord

II. BODY
  A. HE SEES BEYOND THE PLEASANTRIES (v. 41)
    1. "He beheld the city"
    2. So much in the world is superficial
      a. Beautiful Jerusalem, the breathtaking view
      b. The pomp and ceremony of the occasion
    3. But Jesus sees beyond this outward beauty
      a. What He sees makes Him weep
      b. Is He grieved at what He sees in your life?
    4. He sees beyond the outward in a church, "I know thy works" (Rev. 2:2)
    5. He sees beyond the outward in our lives
      a. The facade that hides inward sin
      b. The smile that hides inward tears
  B. HE CARES ABOUT OUR PAIN (v. 41)
    1. ". . . and wept over it"
    2. Was not His primary concern over their sin?
    3. Yes . . . but sin brings pain
      a. From the first sin in the Garden of Eden

        b. Every act of disobedience brings pain

        c. All sin has negative consequences

    4. Do you think you are getting away with sin?

    5. You cannot sin and win

        a. The books you are reading, the lust you tolerate

        b. The words you say, the stories you tell, the lies

        c. All these bring pain

C. HE KNOWS OUR FULL POTENTIAL (v. 42)

    1. "If thou hadst known . . ."

    2. What Jerusalem might have been:

        a. The city of blessing

        b. Instead it has become a city of war and grief

    3. Jesus knows your full potential

        a. The saddest words of tongue or pen: "It might have been"

        b. He knows what you can achieve. Don't underestimate Him

    4. Have you blown it? A great future beats a great past every time

D. HE LONGS TO GIVE US PEACE (v. 42)

    1. "The things which belong to thy peace"

    2. Peace! What a good word it is! REPEAT IT!!!

    3. Jerusalem means city of peace

    4. But war was waiting in the wings (vv. 43, 44) . . . Titus and fulfillment of this prophecy

III. CONCLUSION

    A. PREACH THE GOSPEL

    B. PEACE FOR INDIVIDUALS . . . COME NOW!

    C. YOUR TEARS CAN CHANGE TO JOY

SUBMISSION

Luke 19:28–40

I. INTRODUCTION
   A. PALM SUNDAY
      1. So called because of the palm branches used
      2. The triumphal entry
      3. Recorded by all the Gospel writers
   B. THE SETTING AND THE SCENE
      1. About five days before Passover
      2. Jesus and the disciples come from Bethany
      3. Most important of all the Jewish feasts was about to begin
      4. Probably 300,000 pilgrims there for the Passover
   C. OUR ATTENTION FROM THE CELEBRATING MULTI-TUDE TO THE SUBMITTED MINORITY. NOTE THAT THEIR ACCOMPLISHMENTS ARE STILL IMPORTANT TODAY

II. BODY
   A. THE SUBMISSION OF JESUS TO THE WILL OF THE FATHER (v. 28)
      1. "Ascending up to Jerusalem"
      2. There was danger in that statement
         a. The attempt on His life before at Jerusalem (John 10:22–40)
         b. After Lazarus was raised, the danger increased
      3. There was fulfillment of prophecy in it
         a. Zechariah 9:9: Christ riding into Jerusalem on a donkey
         b. Daniel 9:25: Christ to arrive as the Prince on that day
      4. There was submission to the Father's will in it
         a. This would lead to the cross . . . His reason for coming
         b. Ahead would be the last supper . . . the first communion . . . the trial . . . the scourging . . . the cross

     5. Consider the submission of Christ described in Philippians 2:5–7

B. THE SUBMISSION OF THE DISCIPLES TO THE WILL OF THE SAVIOR (vv. 29–35)

    1. The strange instruction to the disciples about the colt

    2. The disciples must submit their wills to obey

       a. "Go Ye." The word of Christ the same today, "Go!"

       b. "To the village over against you." Begin at home

       c. "Ye shall find a colt." Jesus knows all about our tomorrows

       d. "A colt tied." The bondage of sin. Go to those who are tied

       e. "Whereon never man sat." An unbroken will

       f. "Loose him." Free him from all that binds him

       g. "Bring him hither." Bring those who are bound to Jesus

       h. "If any ask." There will always be public opinion

       i. "The Lord hath need of him." Finally, a purpose in life

    3. Many out there waiting to be freed

C. THE SUBMISSION OF THE DONKEY TO THE CREATOR AND KING (vv. 35–40)

    1. They brought him to Jesus

    2. They cast their garments on him

    3. Jesus was set thereupon

    4. The stubborn will of the donkey submitted to Jesus

    5. Jesus and nature: Storms, winds, the sea, fish, rocks subject to His will

    6. A picture of the coming kingdom (Isa. 11:6–8)

III. CONCLUSION

A. IS YOUR WILL SUBMITTED TO HIS WILL?

B. SUBMISSION IN THE CHRISTIAN LIFE: TO ONE ANOTHER, WIVES TO HUSBANDS, CITIZENS TO LAWS, BELIEVERS TO CHURCH LEADERS

C. THE CALL TO SURRENDER

FROM MORTICIANS TO MISSIONARIES

Luke 24:8–9

I. INTRODUCTION
  A. THE CROSS AND ITS RESULTS
    1. The priests—rid of the One who spoke with such authority
    2. The Pharisees—rid of Him whose life revealed their sin
    3. The authorities—rid of the tumult with the people
    4. Peter—boastful before, but broken now
    5. Joseph of Arimathea—cowardly before, but courageous now
  B. THE SETTING AND THE SCENE, IMPACT UPON THE WOMEN
    1. The women make their way to the tomb to embalm the Lord's body
    2. The first day of the week, the Lord's day
    3. Very early in the morning, the first sunrise service
    4. The stone rolled away, they had worried about the safekeeping of Jesus' body

II. BODY
  A. THE WOMEN REMEMBERED HIS WORDS (vv. 6–8)
    1. The question, "Why seek ye the living among the dead?"
      a. A good question for today
      b. A good question for those with loved ones in heaven
    2. He is not here!
      a. Don't look for the Savior in the cemetery
      b. He lives. He is risen
      c. "I am he that liveth and was dead and am alive again" (Rev. 1:18)
    3. The great injunction: REMEMBER
      a. Matthew 12:40; Matthew 20:18; Matthew 26:2
      b. The prophesies of His coming death
    4. And they remembered

        a. Do you remember how He first spoke to you about your need of salvation?

        b. Perhaps the most important thing that could happen to you

B. THE WOMEN RETURN TO THE OTHERS (v. 9)

  1. How differently they return

  2. The state of their hearts as they arrived

        a. Sad, discouraged, doubtful

        b. Every step had said: He is dead

        c. They came to anoint His body, to do the work of undertakers, but found GOD HAD UNDERTAKEN

  3. The change as they return

        a. The quick step, the excited heart

        b. What a difference when you know that He lives!

  4. You need to remember and return to Him

C. THE WOMEN REPORT (v. 9)

  1. "And told all these things to the rest"

  2. Imagine the excitement

  3. What a change! They went to be *morticians*, but they returned as *missionaries*

  4. They went to that tomb with their hands full of spices; they returned with their hearts filled with songs and their mouths filled with sermons

  5. They went to anoint a body and returned to announce a blessing

  6. The greatest message the world has ever heard

III. CONCLUSION

A. THE NEED OF THOSE TO WHOM THEY SPOKE

  1. Poor backslidden Peter

  2. Heartbroken John, a discouraged, doubting band of disciples

B. THE RISEN CHRIST WILL MEET YOUR NEED

THE RISEN CHRIST . . . WHAT IS HE LIKE?

Luke 24:13–32

I. INTRODUCTION
  A. THE GREAT DAY OF VICTORY
    1. The day of the resurrection, never a day like this
    2. Strangely, doubted by His disciples, believed by His enemies
  B. WHAT IS CHRIST LIKE SINCE HIS RESURRECTION?
    1. His humble birth, His compassionate life, so approachable
    2. Weeping over Jerusalem, at a grave, silent at trial, caring in death
    3. What now?
  C. LET US VIEW THE RISEN CHRIST AS HE COMMUNICATES WITH MEN

II. BODY
  A. HE IS THE CHRIST WHO WALKS WITH MEN (v. 15)
    1. The depressed disciples returning home to Emmaus
    2. That same day
      a. A day for rejoicing, but they are retreating
      b. A day for triumph, but they are trembling
      c. A day for shouting and singing, but they are sad
    3. Then Christ drew near and walked with them
      a. Resurrection has not made Him remote
      b. Triumph has not changed His tenderness
    4. Went with them in the way
  B. HE IS THE CHRIST WHO CARES FOR THE PROBLEMS OF MEN (vv. 17–25)
    1. Note His question to them, "What communications . . . Why sad?"
    2. He knew, but wanted them to tell Him . . . just as today
    3. Here is their problem: They think He is dead
    4. Notice that it is His disciples who are in this depressed state

67

a. We, also, are often guilty
b. We mope and dread as if God were dead
c. We fret and stew as if God were through
d. We moan and groan as if God were not on the throne
e. We weakly pray as if God were away

5. But He lives and we ought to remember it!

C. HE IS THE CHRIST WHO SETS THE HEARTS OF MEN ON FIRE (v. 32)

1. How their hearts needed rekindling!
2. Once they had expected great things from Christ. Now they just say nice things about Him
3. Once they had expected Him to perform the greatest miracle. Now they doubt His resurrection
4. They were slow of heart to believe
   a. Once they were thrilled, now they are chilled
   b. They remember a better day
5. Notice how Jesus set their hearts on fire
   a. He took them to the Bible
   b. He showed them His wounded hands
6. Is your heart on fire for Christ?

III. CONCLUSION

A. HEARTS ON FIRE . . . CHANGED LIVES

1. Changed their direction
2. Made them seek out a gathering of other Christians
3. Gave them assurance of His power

B. NEEDED: HEARTS ON FIRE FOR GOD!

"BUTS" OF THE RESURRECTION

I Corinthians 15

I. INTRODUCTION
  A. THERE IS ONLY ONE QUESTION ABOUT LIFE, DEATH, AND ETERNITY
    1. Is Christ risen?
    2. The question of the Pharisees
      a. "What sign showest thou?" (John 2:18)
      b. "Destroy this temple, and in three days I will raise it up" (John 12:19)
  B. THE GREATEST CHAPTER ON THE RESURRECTION
    1. Paul's letter to a troubled church
      a. Divisions, carnality, immorality, confusion, and victory
      b. Paul ends his letter with truth about resurrection
    2. Three verses, (13, 20, 57), all beginning with the same word — BUT

II. BODY
  A. BUT . . . IF THERE BE NO RESURRECTION (v. 13)
    1. The frightening prospect of no resurrection
    2. "What-ifs" of history
      a. Christopher Columbus had not made his voyage
      b. Martin Luther had not dared stand for truth
      c. Adolph Hitler had pushed his advantage and taken England
    3. Perhaps you have some "What-if" of life that frightens you
    4. None compare with this: "but if no resurrection?"
      a. All preaching would be vain
        (1) Great sermons of Paul and other apostles
        (2) Great preachers of the ages: Wesley, John Knox, Spurgeon, Moody, etc.
        (3) Write them off as useless
      b. All faith is vain . . . empty . . . useless
        (1) Faith is trust . . . dependence

          (2) Faith brings salvation . . . blessing

      c. Ye are yet in your sins

      d. The dead are perished . . . no hope of heaven

  B. BUT . . . NOW IS CHRIST RISEN FROM THE DEAD (v. 20)

    1. The shout of triumph: He lives!

    2. No more "ifs"

    3. Therefore, all the former has meaning

      a. Gospel preaching is true

      b. Faith is sure . . . brings salvation . . . dependable

      c. Sins are forgiven . . . the record is clear . . . the load lifted

      d. Christians go to heaven when they die and will be resurrected when Jesus returns

    4. Suppose it's all true! IT IS ALL TRUE: Christ is risen!

  C. BUT THANKS BE TO GOD WHO GIVETH US THE VICTORY (v. 57)

    1. Dangling again for a time

    2. Death . . . the grave . . . sin . . . law

    3. But Christians are not bound

      a. Victory over death

      b. Victory over sin

      c. Victory over the law

      d. Victory over the grave

    4. What a great day! What a great message!

III. CONCLUSION

  A. THEREFORE . . . (v. 58)

    1. Responsibility follows truth

    2. Always abounding

  B. ACT ON POSITIVE TRUTH. LEAVE THE NEGATIVES BEHIND

THE MOST VALUABLE MEN IN TOWN

Acts 4:12–14

I. INTRODUCTION
   A. THE PRIESTS AND THEIR EVALUATION OF PETER AND JOHN
      1. Called them ignorant and unlearned
      2. They would do more to change the world than all in Jerusalem
      3. Thirteen men who changed the world
         a. One doctor, one intellectual, and the rest unlettered
         b. Look at a map of the world and see the impact of their lives
   B. WHY THEY WERE THE MOST VALUABLE MEN IN TOWN
II. BODY
   A. THEY WERE NOT UNLEARNED AND IGNORANT ABOUT THE SAVIOR (v. 10)
      1. They had been with Jesus
      2. The world needs people who have been with Jesus
         a. Many know about science, but few know the Savior
         b. Many know about mathematics, but few know about the Master
         c. Many know about space, but few know about grace
         d. Many know about politics, but few know about God's plan
         e. Many know about psychology, but few know the One who solves all problems
      3. The mystery to the priests
         a. The educational background of these fishermen
         b. Suddenly they were public speakers and theologians
      4. What God will do with one who is completely surrendered to Him
   B. THEY WERE NOT UNLEARNED AND IGNORANT ABOUT THE SCRIPTURES (vv. 10–12)
      1. The knowledge explosion

71

2. Sadly our increased knowledge has but deepened our dilemma
3. These men did not know books, but they knew the Book
   a. Lincoln: "Better to have a knowledge of the Bible than other books"
   b. Their knowledge of the Bible equipped them to serve
4. Most great universities in America founded to teach the Bible
   a. Man foolishly gets too wise for God's Book
   b. Psalm 2: "He that sitteth in the heavens shall laugh"
5. These men had a knowledge of the Old Testament
6. Their knowledge of the Bible let them know what was happening

C. THEY WERE NOT UNLEARNED AND IGNORANT ABOUT SALVATION (v. 12)
1. "Salvation"—The importance of the word
2. To Noah, the ark meant salvation while others perished
3. To Israel at the Red Sea: "Stand still and see the salvation of the Lord" (Exod. 14:13)
4. People are trapped by problems and perplexed
   a. These men could tell people how to get rid of their sins
   b. These men could tell people how to get to heaven

III. CONCLUSION
   A. YOU CAN BE THE MOST VALUABLE PERSON IN YOUR AREA
   B. THE NEED IS GREAT. GIVE YOUR LIFE TO CHRIST FOR HIS SERVICE
      1. Take time to be with Jesus
      2. Saturate your mind and heart with the Bible
      3. Carry the message of salvation to others
   C. GOD WILL USE YOU TO CHANGE YOUR WORLD

CHRISTIANS IN CONFLICT

1 *Corinthians* 6

I. INTRODUCTION
   A. FIRST CORINTHIANS IS A VERY PRACTICAL BOOK
      1. While not giving much space to doctrine, it deals with life
      2. Meets the Christian in his day-to-day relationship with other believers
         a. Morality . . . malice . . . money
         b. Bickering . . . backbiting . . . spiritual babyhood
   B. CONFLICTS THAT CALL FOR COURT ACTION
      1. Believers going to court
      2. Does this apply today? Yes!
   C. QUESTIONS TO HANDLE CHRISTIAN CONFLICT

II. BODY
   A. A QUESTION ABOUT THE CONSEQUENCE OF CHRISTIAN CONFLICTS (v. 1)
      1. "Dare any of you . . . go to law before the unjust?"
      2. Think of the testimony before others when Christians cannot get along
      3. Think of the loss of blessing when Christians are in conflict
      4. Think about the crippling of all soul-winning efforts when Christians use their energies in conflict
      5. Think about the accountability of your effort and time
      6. The word to David after his sin: "You have given cause to the enemies of God to rejoice" (2 Sam. 12:1-14)
   B. QUESTIONS ABOUT THE COMPETENCE OF CHRISTIANS TO SETTLE DIFFERENCES (vv. 2-5)
      1. "Do ye not know that the saints shall judge the world?"
      2. See Daniel 7:22 and Matthew 19:28
      3. "And if the world shall be judged by you are ye unworthy to judge the smallest matters?"
      4. "Know ye not that we shall judge angels" (presumably evil ones)
      5. "How much more the things that pertain to this life?"

      6. "If then, ye have judgments of things pertaining to this life, set them to judge who are least esteemed in the church?"

  C. QUESTIONS THAT COULD KILL THE COURSE OF CONFLICT?

      1. "Why do ye not rather take wrong?" (v. 7)

         a. In so doing we diffuse a bad situation

         b. Like Jesus (1 Peter 2:23, 24)

      2. "Why do ye not rather allow yourselves to be defrauded?"

         a. Defrauded: See 1 Corinthians 7:5

         b. Let another have what is rightfully yours

      3. The secret is Philippians 2:5–11

III. CONCLUSION

  A. WHAT ARE YOUR AREAS OF CONFLICT?

  B. TAKE WRONG AND GLORIFY GOD

ETERNAL LOVE

1 Corinthians 13

I. INTRODUCTION
   A. THOUGHTS ABOUT LOVE
      1. Remembering God's great love to us
      2. The cross: the greatest demonstration of God's love
      3. The problem at Corinth: A lack of love
   B. THE POWER OF LOVE
      1. Love conquers all bickering and brings blessing
      2. Love builds fellowship and restores faith
      3. Love draws together and brings lost sinners to salvation

II. BODY
   A. THE POWERLESSNESS OF SERVICE WITHOUT LOVE (vv. 1–3)
      1. The whole gospel message is God's great love story
      2. *Speaking Without Love Is Just Noise*
         a. No matter how you speak—you are weak without love
         b. No matter your words—they are worthless without love
         c. No matter how sincere—you will fail without love
      3. *Spiritual Gifts Without Love are Just Nothing*
         a. The gift of prophecy: Knowing the future
         b. The gift of understanding: All the mysteries
         c. The gift of knowledge: Knowledge of God's will
         d. The gift of faith: Power to move mountains
      4. *Sacrifice Without Love Is Just Nonsense*
         a. Bestow all my goods to feed the poor
         b. Give my body to be burned
   B. THE PRACTICAL EFFECTS OF LOVE (vv. 4–7)
      1. Love suffereth long (love reacting): Puts up with many things
         a. Peter: "How many times shall I forgive?"
         b. What small things can shake and break us!

    2. Love is kind. The positive side

    3. Love envieth not. Envy springs from catering to self

    4. Love vaunteth not itself. Is not puffed up

    5. Does not behave itself unseemly. Seeketh not her own

    6. Is not easily provoked. Not irritable

    7. Thinketh no evil. Hardly notices when others do it wrong

    8. Rejoiceth not in iniquity. Never glad about injustice

    9. Rejoiceth in the truth. Beareth all things

  10. Believeth all things. Instead of looking for little faults, love expects the best

C. THE PERMANENCE OF LOVE (vv. 8–13)

    1. Love never faileth. Will not get obsolete

    2. Prophecy to fail

    3. Tongues to cease

    4. Even the special gift of knowledge to disappear

    5. Not love. It remains

III. CONCLUSION

A. THE FRUIT OF THE SPIRIT IS LOVE (Gal. 5:22–23)

B. FULL SURRENDER TO THE HOLY SPIRIT PRODUCES THIS LOVE IN US

A WOMAN TO REMEMBER IN THE LAST DAYS

Luke 17:32

I. INTRODUCTION
   A. AN END-TIME SETTING
      1. The days of Noah
      2. The days of Lot
      3. The suddenness of the Lord's coming
   B. LOT'S WIFE CHOSEN AS A WARNING TO THOSE WHO LIVE IN THE LAST DAYS
      1. Why Lot's wife?
      2. Why not Sarah, Hannah, Ruth or Mary?
      3. What does Lot's wife have to say about the end time?
   C. WHAT SHALL WE REMEMBER ABOUT THIS WOMAN?

II. BODY
   A. LET US REMEMBER HER RELIGIOUS PRIVILEGES
      1. She had shared the experiences of Abraham
         a. His call and his move of faith (Gen. 12)
         b. His altar and his prayer life
         c. His giving and his generosity toward her and her family
      2. She had a righteous husband (2 Peter 2:7–8)
      3. We live in a day of religious privilege
         a. Churches available almost everywhere
         b. Radio and television ministries
         c. An abundant supply of Bibles
         d. Many great literature ministries
      4. Religious privilege does not save
         a. Gehazi was the servant of Elisha
         b. Demas was the associate of Paul
         c. Judas was a disciple of Christ
      5. The last days to be characterized by wickedness in spite of much light (Matt. 24:12)
   B. LET US REMEMBER THE PRAYERS OF HER RELATIVE
      1. Abraham undoubtedly prayed for her and Lot many times

77

   2. Consider Abraham's intercession for Sodom to be
      spared (Gen. 18)
      a. These prayers brought angels to Sodom
      b. These prayers brought her potential deliverance
   3. Many have relatives faithfully praying for them
      a. Perhaps you have a father or mother praying for
          you
      b. Your wife or husband may be often in prayer for
          you
   4. Churches and prayer groups around the world
      a. Pleading for souls
      b. Naming loved ones before the throne of grace
C. LET US REMEMBER HER PERISHING
   1. In the midst of her possessions and privileges, she
      perished
   2. Her lot became that of her treasures; they perished
   3. What her looking back revealed
      a. It revealed her disobedience
      b. It revealed her unbelief
      c. It revealed her bondage to the things of this world
   4. Her death was sudden and shocking
      a. She died much as she lived
      b. She died in an act of sin

III. CONCLUSION
   A. WE TOO LIVE IN A DOOMED PLACE: THIS WORLD
   B. A WARNING FROM PETER IN LIGHT OF THIS (2 Peter
       3:11)
   C. LEARN FROM LOT'S WIFE
       1. Turn from passing things to eternal ones
       2. Get ready for the return of our Lord

IF JESUS SHOULD COME TODAY

1 *Thessalonians* 4:13–18; 1 *John* 2:28

I. INTRODUCTION
  A. JESUS IS COMING AGAIN
    1. The One who died and rose again will come again
    2. Millions accept this truth intellectually
    3. Relatively few allow this to change their lives
      a. This may be the strangest fact of history
      b. How would you adjust your life if you knew Christ would come today?
  B. SIGNS THAT MAKE US FEEL THE COMING OF THE LORD IS NEAR
    1. Israel is a nation (Ezek. 37)
    2. Russia is a militaristic world power with designs on the Middle East (Ezek. 38—39)
    3. The world is getting ready for the Antichrist (Rev. 13)
    4. Signs in nature (Matt. 24:7)
  C. WHAT WILL HAPPEN WHEN JESUS COMES?
II. BODY
  A. IF JESUS SHOULD COME TODAY, THE CHRISTIAN DEAD WOULD BE RAISED (4:13–16)
    1. The sound of the trumpet . . . the voice of the archangel
    2. The dead in Christ rise first (WONDERFUL HOPE!)
      a. The grave is not a place of despair
      b. Christians go to heaven when they die (2 Cor. 5:8)
      c. The Lord returns bringing Christians with Him to resurrect their bodies
    3. This resurrection means a reunion of body, soul, and spirit
    4. The new body will be like the body of Christ (1 John 3:2)
      a. No more sickness, pain, or suffering
      b. No more death
      c. No more limitations
  B. IF JESUS SHOULD COME TODAY, LIVING BELIEVERS WOULD ESCAPE DEATH (4:15–17)
    1. Death has taken its toll through the centuries

        a. Adam died and Abel died

        b. Methusalah died and Moses died

        c. Jacob died and Joseph died

    2. Samson was not strong enough to escape death

    3. Solomon was not wise enough to escape death

    4. Men still die (Heb. 9:27)

    5. But not all Christians will die

        a. Those living when Jesus comes will be caught up and changed

        b. "We shall not all sleep" (1 Cor. 15:51)

    6. Like Enoch and Elijah, all believers living when Christ comes will be changed (translated) without death

    7. What a blessed hope!

  C. IF JESUS SHOULD COME TODAY, SOME WOULD BE ASHAMED (1 John 2:28)

    1. Abiding in Him that we may have confidence

    2. Are you confident when thinking of His return?

    3. The suddenness of His coming . . . in a moment

        a. When you were in that fit of anger

        b. When you were reading that borderline book

        c. When you were passing on that bit of gossip

    4. This is a solemn truth for believers

    5. Be ready for His coming

III. CONCLUSION

  A. THE RETURN OF CHRIST A BLESSED AND SOBERING EVENT

  B. ARE YOU WILLING TO LET THIS TRUTH CHANGE YOUR LIFE?

THE MOTHER WHO STRUCK OIL AT HOME

2 Kings 4:1−7

I. INTRODUCTION
  A. MOTHERS AND THEIR MANY RESPONSIBILITIES
    1. Who can number them all?
    2. Yet mothers are equipped by God for this task
    3. Motherhood was the first command of God to Eve
  B. THE ADDED RESPONSIBILITIES OF WIDOWHOOD
    1. The increased load when the husband is gone
    2. Such is the case in the text before us

II. BODY
  A. THIS MOTHER KNEW WHERE TO GO IN THE TIME OF NEED (v. 1)
    1. The preacher's widow
      a. Wife of one of the sons of the prophets
      b. About this departed preacher
        (1) Must have been a man of faith. Served under Elisha
        (2) Must have been fearless. He didn't have any money
        (3) Must have been hard working. He died young
    2. The problems: Death and debts
      a. The two great burdens of life
      b. The creditor comes to foreclose on the boys to be bondmen
    3. The widow went quickly to seek the wisdom and help of God
    4. Blessed is the mother who knows where to go when her family is in need
  B. THIS MOTHER FOUND THE ANSWER TO HER NEED WAS RIGHT AT HOME (vv. 2−4)
    1. Elisha considering her problem: "What shall I tell thee?"
    2. Elisha's searching question: "What hast thou in the house?"

        a. A good question for all mothers today
        b. A husband who loves you? Food enough for today?
        c. Money for this week's groceries?
        d. This mother had none of these things
    3. The negative answer: "Thy handmaid hath not any-
        thing"
        a. Mothers and others with this attitude are miserable
        b. "Others get new things, I am deprived. Poor me!"
    4. THE STARTLING DISCOVERY: "SAVE A LITTLE POT
        OF OIL." A POSITIVE MOVE
        a. Literally "an anointing of oil"
        b. But this was the turning point
        c. How long has it been since you counted your
            blessings?
        d. Rediscovering the house, the family, the furniture,
            love
    5. The answer for lifting your burden may be right at
        home
  C. THIS MOTHER FOUND THAT THE POSSIBILITIES ARE
      UNLIMITED WHEN YOU ALLOW GOD TO USE WHAT
      YOU HAVE (vv. 4–7)
    1. Heeding the message of Elisha in faith
    2. Involving her sons in the act of faith
        a. Sent them borrowing
        b. Thinking big! "Borrow not a few"
        c. Expecting the answer
    3. The closed doors. The thrilling moment
        a. God took what she had and multiplied it
        b. Filling all the borrowed vessels
    4. What God will do with what you have
        a. A boy's lunch
        b. Moses' rod
        c. David's sling
III. CONCLUSION
  A. WHATEVER YOU HAVE IS ENOUGH FOR GOD TO USE
  B. WHAT HAST THOU IN THE HOUSE?
A.B. Simpson: "Our God has boundless resources. The only limit is
in us. Our asking, our thinking, our praying are too small. Our
expectations are too limited."

THE WOMAN OF GREAT FAITH

Matthew 15:21–28

I. INTRODUCTION
   A. MANY WOMEN OF THE BIBLE MIGHT PROVIDE SERMON TEXTS FOR MOTHER'S DAY
      1. The mother of Moses or the mother of Samuel
      2. Mary, the mother of Jesus
   B. I HAVE CHOSEN ALMOST AN UNKNOWN
      1. A woman of great faith
      2. A woman who received an answer to her prayer

II. BODY
   A. A MOTHER REVEALS HER PROBLEM (vv. 21–23)
      1. Many troubled mothers in the world
      2. Some things about this mother
         a. She was a Canaanite, a Syro-Phonecian
         b. By culture and language a Greek
         c. By religion up until now a pagan. THIS DAY A CHANGE
      3. Her greatest problem had to do with her daughter
         a. She had other problems, but they seemed small
         b. The high fever . . . the anxious hours in crisis
         c. To the normal parent all problems seem small when their children are at stake
      4. Her daughter was greviously vexed with a devil (a demon)
         a. The most distressing of all parental problems is the devil's attack on their children
         b. The importance of praying for protection from Satan's attacks on family members
   B. A MOTHER REMAINS PERSISTENT IN PRAYER (vv. 22–27)
      1. She came to Jesus with her problem. Blessed is the woman who knows where to go with her problems
      2. She believed everything about Jesus
         a. She believed He was the promised son of David

83

         b. She believed in His deity

         c. She believed in His power to answer her request

         d. She believed He was interested and would answer

     3. The problems confronting her answer

         a. Jesus didn't answer at first

         b. The disciples wanted her sent away

     4. Her persistence in spite of discouragement

         a. Her worship

         b. Her simple prayer

         c. The Lord's strange statements

         d. The Lord testing her faith

         e. A dog at the table

   C. A MOTHER RECEIVES A PROMISE FROM THE LORD (v. 28)

     1. O woman, great is thy faith

         a. Better than great is thy beauty

         b. Better than great is thy professional success

         c. Better than great is thy influence

     2. Her daughter was made whole from that very hour

III. CONCLUSION

   A. COME TO JESUS WITH YOUR PROBLEMS ABOUT YOUR CHILDREN

   B. THE WORLD COULD BE CHANGED BY WOMEN OF GREAT FAITH

HOW TO WIN YOUR HUSBAND, TREAT YOUR WIFE, AND GET YOUR PRAYERS ANSWERED

1 Peter 3:1–7

I. INTRODUCTION
   A. THE AIM OF THE BIBLE IS TO BRING YOU SALVATION
      1. This purpose is seen from Genesis to Revelation
      2. This chapter also aims at any unsaved in the home
   B. BUT THE BIBLE AIMS AT THE WHOLE NEED OF THE WHOLE MAN
      1. How to win your husband to Christ
      2. How to treat your wife
      3. How to get your prayers answered

II. BODY
   A. HOW TO WIN YOUR HUSBAND TO CHRIST (vv. 1–6)
      1. Peter brings us a very real problem
      2. The picture of a woman of the first century trying to win her husband to Christ
      3. Important that youth see the importance of marrying Christians
      4. Also important that Christian wives see the importance of staying with husbands as faithful witnesses (1 Cor. 7:13, 14)
      5. Be in subjection to your husband
         a. Not a slave, but not a rebel
         b. Not a domineering woman (Prov. 14:1; 19:13; 21:9, 19)
      6. If any obey not the word: literally, non-persuadable
      7. Without the word: not through preaching
      8. Chaste conversation: pure behavior and respect
      9. You cannot win your husband:
         a. By the way you fix your hair
         b. By surprising him with loads of jewelry
         c. By wearing a particular kind of clothing
      10. A meek and quiet spirit

        a. Something really expensive in the sight of God

        b. A spiritual woman, then, is not loud

        c. Not how loud she can be in church with Amens

        d. But how much love she can show at home with her man

   11. The example of Sarah, who called him Lord

B. HOW TO TREAT YOUR WIFE (v. 7)

   1. LIKEWISE - Note that, all you men who have been saying, "Amen"

   2. In an intelligent and reasonable manner

   3. Honor as to the weaker vessel

        a. What a privilege to provide for your wife!

        b. What a privilege to be the protector of your wife!

        c. Woman from Adam's rib

   4. Heirs together of the grace of life

        a. One in God's sight

        b. The grace of life, eternal life that comes by grace

C. HOW TO GET YOUR PRAYERS ANSWERED

   1. "That your prayers not be hindered"

   2. A wrong relationship between husband and wife can hinder prayers

   3. "If two of you shall agree on earth as touching anything" (Matt. 18:19, 20)

   4. How wonderful that can be for husband and wife!

   5. The power of praying families in a church

III. CONCLUSION

A. SINCE CHRIST SUFFERED FOR US HE KNOWS THE DIFFICULT CIRCUMSTANCES WE FACE

B. HE ORDAINED THE HOME AND WANTS TO PRESERVE IT

C. A CALL FOR CHRIST-CENTERED HOMES

BUILDING A STRONG MARRIAGE

Psalm 127; 1 Corinthians 13

I. INTRODUCTION
  A. THE BREAKDOWN OF THE AMERICAN HOME
    1. "Doesn't anybody stay together anymore?"
    2. What can be done about it?
  B. SOME BASIC BIBLICAL TRUTHS TO MAKE A DIFFER-ENCE

II. BODY
  A. A STRONG MARRIAGE IS BUILT UPON THE LORD (Ps. 127:1)
    1. "They labor in vain that build it"
      a. Note that they are trying but are sure to fail
      b. All of their efforts are to no avail
    2. Reminds me of Paul's words about the resurrection of Christ
      a. "If Christ be not risen, your faith is vain" (1 Cor. 15:14)
      b. Just like that: A marriage without Christ fails
    3. Building a marriage on the Lord gives a divine dimension to life
      a. Our first day: reading the Bible and praying
      b. A desire to serve the Lord from the start
    4. Building a marriage on the Lord makes a difference when the storms come
      a. Many marriages fall apart when trouble comes
      b. Debts drive many to divorce
      c. But Christians know where to turn when storms rage!
      d. The wise man and the foolish man (Luke 6:47–49)
  B. A STRONG MARRIAGE IS BUILT UPON LOVE (1 Cor. 13:4–6)
    1. Not the kind of love portrayed by Hollywood
    2. God's definition of love as described in 1 Corinthians 13:4–7
    3. The practical effects of love

      a. Love suffereth long . . . is patient . . . not exploding
      b. Love is kind. Are you kind to one another?
          (1) Are you kind in word?
          (2) Are you kind in actions?
      c. Vaunteth not itself, is not puffed up . . . not out for number one
      d. Doesn't behave unseemly . . . not rude
      e. Seeketh not her own . . . not selfish
      f. Is not easily provoked . . . not irritable
      g. Thinketh no evil . . . hardly notices when done wrong and doesn't hold grudges
      h. Rejoiceth not in iniquity . . . not glad about injustice but pleased when truth wins out

C. A STRONG MARRIAGE IS BUILT UPON LOYALTY (1 Cor. 13:7)
   1. Beareth all things . . . loyal even when things are tough
   2. Believeth all things . . . believing in your mate . . . trusting
   3. Hopeth all things . . . expects the best of the loved one
   4. Endureth all things . . . defends when others forsake
   5. Note how all of these things are true in the Lord's love for us
   6. Note how this holds with the divine instruction for the first marriage . . . and those to follow

III. CONCLUSION
  A. YOU CAN HAVE A STRONG MARRIAGE
  B. BUILD ON THE LORD . . . ON LOVE . . . ON LOYALTY
  C. OTHER HOUSES MAY FALL BUT YOURS WILL STAND

GIVE ME THIS MOUNTAIN

Joshua 14:6–14

I. INTRODUCTION
   A. A DAY FOR REMEMBERING AND A DAY FOR PATRIOTISM
      1. Remembering those who have fallen in battle
      2. Remembering all loved ones who have died
   B. A TEXT FROM A BOOK OF BATTLES
      1. After Moses, Joshua became the leader
      2. The land divided among the tribes of Israel
      3. The area given will have to be conquered and developed
   C. CALEB: "GIVE ME THIS MOUNTAIN"
      1. Asks the most difficult task (v. 12)
      2. What motivated Caleb to press on to higher ground?

II. BODY
   A. HE REMEMBERS GOD'S PROMISE TO HIM (vv. 6–7)
      1. Caleb the spy (Num. 13:14)
         a. Sent by Moses 40 years earlier to spy out the land
         b. The fruit of the land, flowing with milk and honey
         c. But Caleb saw beyond this to Hebron, where Abram met God
      2. Caleb: "We are well able to overcome it" (Num. 14:23–24)
         a. The majority had great giants and a little God
         b. Caleb had a great God and little giants
         c. The majority were problem-conscious, but Caleb was power-conscious
      3. Caleb will now stand on the promises
         a. He will never forget them
         b. You will never find him part of the grumbling crowd
         c. He is on his way to this better land all through life
   B. CALEB REMEMBERS HIS OWN COMMITMENT TO THE LORD (vv. 8–9)
      1. "I wholly followed the Lord . . ."

         a. Reminded of the time of his full surrender

         b. A man of God, total dedication, committed

     2. Remembers how he had stood apart from the crowd

         a. Do you remember a day of victory?

         b. What about the day you were saved?

         c. What about the time of full surrender?

     3. The sad story of Revelation 2:1–7

     4. Have you left your first love?

  C. CALEB REMEMBERS GOD'S FAITHFULNESS TO HIM (vv. 10–11)

     1. God hath kept me alive

         a. Have you thanked God for keeping you alive?

         b. Except for Joshua, all the rest had died

     2. I am now fourscore and five years old (85)

         a. Some senior citizen!

         b. Not resting on his laurels

     3. God had cared for him up to that hour

     4. "Grace hath brought me safe thus far"

III. CONCLUSION

  A. NOW, THEREFORE, GIVE ME THIS MOUNTAIN!

     1. Give me your best

     2. Give me your toughest task

  B. REMEMBERING SHOULD CHALLENGE US

     1. Lincoln at Gettysburg

     2. Accept the challenge

  C. MOVE ON TO HIGHER GROUND

THE MAN WITH LAME FEET

2 *Samuel* 9

I. INTRODUCTION
   A. THE SOUNDS OF WAR
      1. One of the marks of the sinfulness of man
      2. Wars and rumors of wars (Matt. 24:6)
      3. A scene with a war setting
   B. THE SETTING UP OF DAVID'S KINGDOM
      1. David's kingdom to be established again
      2. Saul, the first king, had failed
      3. God had touched the heart of a young shepherd, and he had been anointed king
   C. KING DAVID'S QUESTION (v. 1)

II. BODY
   A. THE MAN WITH LAME FEET (vv. 1–3)
      1. The national turmoil . . . Saul's kingdom falling
      2. Mephibosheth, five years old, Jonathan's son, the fall (2 Sam. 4:4)
      3. The man with lame feet pictures all of us
         a. We are lame from a fall (Gen. 3)
         b. We do not walk as we should
      4. How we show our infirmities (Gal. 5:19–21)
      5. The two great distressing problems in Mephibosheth's life
         a. Those awful lame feet
         b. His fear of one day having to face the king (Usually all members of a deposed king's family were killed)
      6. Mephibosheth pictures a sinner hiding, running from God, unhappy
   B. THE KING'S INVITATION TO THE MAN WITH LAME FEET (vv. 4–8)
      1. David sends his servant to bring the man with lame feet to him
         a. That knock finally comes, the one he has dreaded

      b. He is living in Lodebar, the place of no pasture

      c. Doesn't realize the king's invitation is for his good

    2. Why David sought the man with lame feet:

      a. To show him the kindness of God (v. 3)

      b. To get to know him on a first-name basis (v. 6)

      c. To take away his fears (v. 7)

      d. To bless him for Jonathan's sake (v. 7)

      e. To restore to him what he had lost (v. 7)

      f. To give him satisfaction (v. 7)

      g. To give him security (v. 7)

    3. Mephibosheth's surprise . . . like your surprise if you come to Jesus

  C. THE MAN WITH LAME FEET SITTING AT THE KING'S TABLE (vv. 9–13)

    1. The king gave him all that he had lost . . . and that his father had lost (v. 9)

    2. Everything now will be for his good

    3. He will always eat bread at the king's table (v. 10)

    4. He will have the position of one of the king's sons (v. 11)

    5. He dwells now in the king's city, Jerusalem, the city of peace instead of Lodebar, the place of no pasture

    6. He continued to be lame in both his feet (v. 13)

      a. But they were now under the king's table

      b. No one could see them

III. CONCLUSION

  A. GOD SEEKS TO DO YOU KINDNESS FOR JESUS' SAKE

  B. RESPOND TO HIS INVITATION

  C. PLACE YOUR LAME FEET UNDER GOD'S TABLE

THE LORD IS GOOD . . .
TELL IT WHEREVER YOU GO!

Nahum 1:7

I. INTRODUCTION
   A. NAHUM OFTEN COUNTED THE HIGHEST AMONG THE MINOR PROPHETS
      1. Nahum prophesied about the time of Isaiah and Micah
      2. Nahum was a native of Galilee
      3. Capernaum means "Village of Nahum"
      4. Nahum means "comforter"
      5. Primarily a book of prophesied judgment against Ninevah . . . about 150 years after Jonah's revival there
      6. Perhaps best known to some because of 2:3–4 . . . sometimes thought to be a prophecy of the automobile
   B. THE TEXT FOR TODAY
      1. A message of tranquility in a time of trouble
      2. A message of comfort in a time of chaos
      3. A message of peace in a time of peril

II. BODY
   A. THE LORD IS GOOD . . . REVEALS THE PERSONALITY OF THE LORD
      1. What good news! God is good
         a. Not a divine dictator bent on punishment
         b. Not a triune tyrant waiting to pounce on us
      2. The child's prayer: "God is great, God is good" HE IS!
      3. The Lord is good: Creation declares it!
         a. Genesis 1:1–25: Each part of creation speaks of His goodness
         b. Creation's beauty is good
         c. Only humanity fell into sin
      4. The Lord is good: The cross demonstrates it
         a. The greatest evidence of His goodness
         b. The greatest demonstration of His mercy and love
         c. The crucified and risen Christ shows God's goodness

B. A STRONGHOLD IN THE DAY OF TROUBLE...
ANNOUNCES THE PROTECTION OF GOD
1. A place of protection in times of peril
2. The walled cities of long ago
3. The early settlers and their forts
4. America as a place of protection for those fleeing persecution
5. Trouble comes to every life, but the Lord meets us there (John 16:33)
   a. Times of sickness
   b. Times of emotional stress
   c. Times of depression
   d. Times of financial reverses
C. HE KNOWETH THEM THAT TRUST IN HIM...SPEAKS OF A PERSONAL WALK WITH GOD
1. The privilege of being known by God
2. Neither a king nor a president...but the Lord
3. See John 10:1–29
4. I know Him and He knows me
5. Trust is the basis of this close relationship

III. CONCLUSION
A. HOW PERFECTLY THIS FOLLOWS REASON
1. The Lord is good
2. He protects us
3. Therefore, He is worthy of our faith
B. TELL THIS GOOD MESSAGE TO THE WORLD

GOD'S BLESSED MAN

Psalm 1

I. INTRODUCTION
  A. WHO WANTS TO BE BLESSED OF GOD?
    1. Most would answer affirmatively
    2. Your presence here indicates your interest in God's blessing
  B. THE FIRST STEP IN GOD'S WAY OF BLESSING IS SALVATION
    1. This is the message of the entire Bible
    2. There is no formula for blessing that does not begin with faith
    3. Psalm 1 assumes that salvation has taken place
  C. PRESCRIPTION FOR BLESSING

II. BODY
  A. THE DANGERS TO GOD'S BLESSED MAN (v. 1)
    1. There are detours along the way
    2. The threefold danger:
      a. Walking in the counsel of the ungodly
        (1) The ungodly always are ready to give advice
        (2) This may be in the form of literature
        (3) This may be in the form of advertising
        (4) This may be in the form of entertainment
      b. Standing in the way of sinners
        (1) First you listen, then you live
        (2) As the twig is bent
      c. Sitting in the seat of the scornful
        (1) Note the progression: first listened, then adopted the standards, now makes fun of God's standards
        (2) The road of the scornful is always downward
    3. Watch out for these dangers
  B. THE DELIGHT OF GOD'S BLESSED MAN (v. 2)
    1. His delight is in the law of the Lord
    2. He has learned to make God's Word his delight

        a. To some it is boring, but to him it is blessed

        b. To some it is dull, but to him it is delightful

        c. To some it is fantasy, but to him it is food

        d. To some it is information, but to him it is inspiration

    3. But not many will make God's Word their delight

        a. You must move against the tide to do this

        b. You must decide to be in the minority

    4. David's delight (Ps. 119:16, 47, 77)

  C. THE DESTINY OF GOD'S BLESSED MAN (v. 3)

    1. He shall be like a tree planted by the rivers of water

    2. What a beautiful illustration

        a. The tree reaching down its roots into the stream

        b. The river represents the Holy Spirit

    3. This tree brings forth fruit (Gal. 5:22–23)

    4. His leaf shall not wither (his testimony)

    5. In whatsoever he does, he will prosper (Rom. 8:28)

III. CONCLUSION

  A. SEE THE DIFFERENCE BETWEEN THE BLESSED MAN AND THE UNGODLY

    1. The ungodly are not so: refers to all of the above

    2. Like the chaff which is with the grain until the wind blows

    3. The ungodly shall not stand in the judgment

        a. "Stand" is the same as "rise up" (the resurrection, Rev. 20:6)

        b. Neither sinners in the congregation . . . when it is made up

  B. BLESSING OR BLIGHT? WHICH WILL IT BE?

THE PRODIGAL'S FATHER

Luke 15:11–32

I. INTRODUCTION
   A. MY FAVORITE FATHER IN THE BIBLE
      1. Chosen by Jesus to illustrate the Heavenly Father
      2. He must then be the ideal earthly father to study
   B. HE WAS A FATHER OF TWO SONS WHO WERE PRODI-GAL FOR A TIME
      1. The younger was prodigal in choosing the pleasures of sin
      2. The older was prodigal in choosing pride of self
   C. BECAUSE THE FATHER WAS WHAT HE WAS, THE PROD-IGAL BECAME WHAT HE SHOULD BE
      1. The younger son returning and the older in decision
      2. What king of a father was he?

II. BODY
   A. HE WAS AN APPROACHABLE FATHER (vv. 12–18)
      1. The text would seem to give some family history
         a. Seems that the mother of the boys had died
         b. Perhaps at the birth of the youngest son
         c. Perhaps this man had stood at a grave with his two boys
         d. Text also indicates wealth (servants)
      2. The young son's dreams: The far country; what was it like?
         a. Some might have slipped off in the night and ran away
         b. Some might have asked another to intercede
         c. This one feels free to come right to his Father: "Father"
      3. Our HEAVENLY FATHER IS APPROACHABLE. "Come to Him as you are"
      4. The far country . . . RIOTOUS LIVING
         a. Dreamed of great task, but found great temptation
         b. Dreamed of adventure, but instead found agony
         c. Dreamed of prestige, but instead found poverty

97

        d. Dreamed of romance, but instead found rags

        e. Dreamed of happiness, but instead found himself feeding the hogs

    5. This Father was approachable even from the pigpen: "I will arise and go to my father"

B. A FATHER WHO IN HIS SON'S MIND WAS ASSOCIATED WITH HEAVEN (v. 18)

    1. "I have sinned against heaven and before thee"

    2. When he thought of heaven, he thought of his father

    3. When he thought of his father, he thought of heaven

    4. He could not be reminded of God without remembering his father

        a. His father surely was a man who walked with God

        b. What an impression! His son couldn't escape it

        c. The father at prayer, in devotions, in reverent walk

        d. His father was godly. How about you?

C. A FATHER WHO WAS AFFECTIONATE (v. 20)

    1. "Ran and fell on his neck and kissed him"

    2. It's nonsense that manhood calls for coldness

    3. The look of love

        a. The father had been watching for him

        b. He ran to meet him. *Spurgeon:* "out of breath but not out of love"

    4. His son was returning

        a. The time away made no difference

        b. The smell of the swine made no difference

        c. The rags made no difference . . . NOR DID THE EMPTY POCKETS

    5. His son is home, that's all that matters

D. A FATHER WHO WAS ASSURING TO BOTH (vv. 21, 31)

    1. "Bring forth the best robe"

    2. Father should take the problems as God the Father takes them

    3. Your failures have not moved you away from His love. RETURN!

III. CONCLUSION

    A. COME NOW TO THE HEAVENLY FATHER

    B. ARE YOU LIKE HIM?

MEN ON FIRE

Daniel 3

I. INTRODUCTION
   A. DANIEL . . . BOOK OF PROPHECY AND PEOPLE
      1. An outline of the ages
      2. Views of the end time
         a. The triumphal entry
         b. The cross . . . the destruction of Jerusalem
         c. The antichrist . . . the tribulation . . . end-time rulers
      3. But it is also a book of people
         a. Daniel, Shadrach, Meshach, Abednego
         b. Trials and triumphs of men of faith
   B. THREE MEN WHO ARE TRIED BY FIRE
      1. The great image
      2. Bow or burn
      3. They refused to bow . . . but did not burn

II. BODY
   A. THEY WERE DIFFERENT (v. 12)
      1. They regarded not the king, nor his gods, nor his golden image
      2. Our Lord was different
         a. He was righteous in a sinful world
         b. He was light on a dark planet
         c. His teachings demanded a different lifestyle
      3. We are to be different, changed by the power of the gospel
         a. Born-again, new creatures
         b. Changed Corinthians (1 Cor. 6:9–11)
         c. Changed Paul (Phil. 3:7–10)
   B. THEY WERE DARING (v. 16)
      1. "We are not careful to answer thee"
      2. The thrill of new Christianity
         a. Taking new stands
         b. Risking position, job, friends

99

        c. Fresh zeal in soul-winning
    3. Then we become careful
        a. So tactful that we never witness
        b. So tolerant of sin that we compromise with the world
        c. So conservative that we make no advances for Christ
    4. The walk of faith is a daring walk
  C. THEY WERE DEDICATED (vv. 17–18)
    1. He is able to deliver us
    2. But if He does not deliver us, we will still be true
    3. You may be angry with God. He has not come through
        a. He did not save your marriage
        b. He did not heal your loved one
        c. He did not rescue your home from foreclosure
        d. He has not yet provided work
        e. He has not yet saved your children
    4. But notice their total commitment
    5. They are like Job: "Though He slay me, yet will I trust Him" (Job 13:15)
    6. They are like Jesus in Gethsemane

III. CONCLUSION
  A. THEY WERE DELIVERED (vv. 25–27)
    1. And what a deliverance!
        a. Jesus walked with them in the fire
        b. Only the ropes burned off
        c. The smell of fire was not on them
        d. Not even their hair was singed
    2. Why??? Because they were already on fire!
  B. WANTED: MEN ON FIRE!

COMMENCEMENT DAY FOR JOSHUA

Joshua 1:1–9

I. INTRODUCTION
  A. COMMON THOUGHTS ABOUT JOSHUA
    1. He fought the Battle of Jericho
    2. The walls came tumblin' down
  B. MORE IMPORTANT FACTS ABOUT JOSHUA
    1. He was Moses' assistant and even accompanied him to Mt. Sinai
    2. He was one of twelve men chosen as spies to scout the land of Canaan (Num. 13:16)
    3. His name is the same as that of Jesus
      a. The Old Testament equivalent
      b. It means God's salvation
  C. JOSHUA'S GRADUATION DAY
    1. Training time is over
    2. Now the real challenges of life begin

II. BODY
  A. GOD HAD A PLAN FOR JOSHUA'S LIFE (v. 2)
    1. When his mother had held him as a baby in Egypt, he was one of a family of slaves
      a. His future seemed to lie in slavery
      b. Likewise, we are born in slavery to sin
    2. Joshua was delivered from both slavery and death by blood
      a. The Passover night: redemption and freedom (Exod. 12)
      b. We are delivered from bondage and the penalty of sin through the blood of Christ (1 Peter 1:18–19)
    3. Now God's plan for Joshua's life is revealed
      a. Moses dies and Joshua becomes the leader
      b. He had never imagined he would reach such a position
    4. God has a plan for your life, beyond what you think you can attain

        a. It is a good plan

        b. It is a plan you can know

        c. It is a plan you can get in on by total surrender

        d. It is a plan that is available immediately

B. GOD GAVE JOSHUA A PROMISE FOR EVERY SITUATION (v. 5)

    1. "I will not fail thee, nor forsake thee"

    2. What a promise! REPEAT IT!

    3. There would come days when Joshua would need it

        a. The defeat at Ai (Josh. 7)

        b. Your down days have not changed the promise

    4. What a great God we serve!

        a. His love is constant and unconditional

        b. His promises never fail

        c. His presence is never removed

    5. The New Testament promise, Hebrews 13:6

C. GOD'S WORD WAS TO BE THE SECRET OF HIS SUCCESS (v. 8)

    1. There are so many books written

    2. "Of the writing of books there is no end" (Eccl. 12:12)

        a. Some good and some bad

        b. Some dry and some delightful

        c. Some beautiful and some boring

    3. But there is but one Book that reveals God to man

        a. Do you seek salvation? It is in the Bible

        b. Do you seek God's will? It is in the Bible

        c. Do you seek guidance? Seek it in the Bible

III. CONCLUSION

  A. SUMMARY

    1. God has a plan for your life

    2. His promises and His grace are sufficient for every need

    3. His Word can be your food and foundation

  B. WALK WITH GOD AND YOU'LL NEVER WALK ALONE!

BROKEN THINGS

Luke 5:1–11

I. INTRODUCTION
- A. JESUS TEACHING BY THE SEA
  1. The Lake of Gennesaret, the Sea of Galilee
     a. Not large but beautiful
     b. Rolling hills and a narrow beach
  2. The crowds and His boat-pulpit
- B. THE MIRACULOUS DRAUGHT OF FISH
  1. A well-known miracle
  2. The Lordship of Christ and His call to serve
- C. BROKEN THINGS

II. BODY
- A. A BROKEN NET (v. 6)
  1. "And the net broke"
  2. The details of the miracle
     a. Fishing was finished and they were washing their nets
     b. They had toiled all the night and caught nothing
     c. Man's extremity is God's opportunity
     d. Failure to this point is not a factor
     e. "Let down your nets for a draught"
     f. The net broke because of so many fish
  3. What this miracle required:
     a. Action when the goal seemed impossible
     b. Work when fatigue called for rest
     c. Faith when circumstances called for doubt
  4. What this miracle demonstrated:
     a. The Lordship of Christ
     b. God's care for our physical needs
     c. The power of Christ over nature
     d. God's power to bless is greater than our capacity to contain
- B. A BROKEN MAN (v. 8)
  1. "Depart from me for I am a sinful man"
  2. What a strange reaction! Why?

        a. Peter knows that he is in the presence of the Lord

        b. His lack of faith

   3. There are many reasons for repentance

        a. Peter's repentance later after denials

        b. The Lord's call to the church at Ephesus (Rev. 2:5)

        c. What is your reason?

C. A BROKEN PARTNERSHIP (v. 10)

   1. "Who were partners with Simon"

   2. Consider the business possibilities:

        a. Simon Johnson and Associates . . . World's Largest Fisheries

        b. Fish for less from your big fisherman

        c. Cornering the fish market with Christ

   3. One statement changed all that

        a. "From henceforth thou shalt catch men"

           (1) From perch to people

           (2) From sole to souls

        b. People are the most important to the Lord

   4. Leaving their boats (v. 11): a picture of surrender

III. CONCLUSION

   A. WHAT MUST YOU LEAVE TO SURRENDER?

   B. LET CHRIST MAKE YOU A FISHER OF MEN

THE UNASWERABLE QUESTION

Hebrews 2:3

I. INTRODUCTION
   A. THERE ARE SOME QUESTIONS TO WHICH THERE IS NO ANSWER
      1. How deep is the bottomless pit?
      2. How wide is space?
      3. How long is eternity?
   B. HOW SHALL WE ESCAPE IF WE NEGLECT SO GREAT SALVATION?
   C. A QUESTION THAT PROMPTS OTHER QUESTIONS

II. BODY
   A. WHAT IS SALVATION?
      1. Salvation is deliverance from the penalty of sin
         a. Once, hell and judgment loomed ahead
         b. Once, every moment moved you closer to destruction
         c. Now, every heartbeat brings you closer to heaven
      2. Salvation is deliverance from the power of sin
         a. Once you were a slave to habits and lust
         b. Now you are free to conquer in the power of God
      3. Salvation is deliverance from the presence of sin
         a. Now surrounded with sin's reality
         b. Man moans about it but chooses it, revels in it, wallows in it
      4. We all need salvation because all have sinned
   B. WHAT IS SO GREAT ABOUT SALVATION?
      1. The price paid for our salvation was great
      2. The fact that all can be saved is great
      3. The simplicity of the messge is great
      4. The changed life is great
      5. The fellowship of the saved is great
      6. The faithfulness of the Savior is great
      7. The fact that this is the one permanent thing in life is great

105

    C. FROM WHAT DO WE ESCAPE IF WE ACCEPT THIS GREAT SALVATION?
        1. How shall we escape?
           a. There is no escape
           b. Even God doesn't know an escape for man
        2. The tragedy of life's neglected opportunites
           a. The job you could have taken
           b. The education you could have received
           c. The property you could have purchased
        3. Picture standing at judgment regretting your neglect
        4. But the man who accepts salvation escapes the following:
           a. The guilt of the past
           b. The fear of the future
           c. Hell
           d. Lake of fire
           e. Tribulation period
           f. Earth's most awful war
           g. The judgment of the Great White Throne

III. CONCLUSION
    A. THE GREAT ESCAPE
    B. ESCAPE TO JESUS

TO HELL AND BACK

Luke 16:19–31

I. INTRODUCTION
   A. A FEARFUL AND OFTEN FORSAKEN PART OF THE BIBLE
      1. Fearful because of the subject involved
      2. Fearful because of the speaker . . . Christ
         a. Could be overlooked if the rantings of a madman
         b. Could be ignored if the folly of a religious fanatic
         c. Could be ignored if but the brainstorm of a bigot
      3. But these words fall from the lips of the gentle Jesus . . . the One who would die and rise again . . . the One who is coming again
   B. THE PRESENTATION IS A STUDY IN CONTRASTS

II. BODY
   A. THE CONTRAST OF THEIR LIVES (vv. 19–21)
      1. A certain rich man . . . he was very rich
         a. Purple . . . a rare and precious die . . . purple spoke of royalty
         b. Fine linen . . . worth twice its weight in gold
         c. Fared sumptuously every day . . . never in doubt as to daily bread
         d. May have even been a religious man but was lost
      2. A certain beggar named Lazarus
         a. Jesus calls His own sheep by name (John 10:3)
         b. Some things we don't know about the beggar
            (1) Don't know his age
            (2) Don't know how long he had been a beggar
         c. Speculation concerning former success
      3. What a contrast for the public to see
      4. But there were some things the public could not see
         a. Did not know the peace Lazarus had
         b. Did not know the emptiness within the heart of the rich man
   B. THE CONTRAST OF THEIR DEATHS (v. 22)
      1. "And the beggar died"

107

    2. Lazarus died first. That was no surprise
       a. But the hours of death can often be surprising
       b. The frailty and yet the endurance of our bodies
       c. No mention of a funeral or burial here at all
       d. Perhaps some potter's field or the valley of Hinnom
    3. The rich man died also
       a. That was a surprise!
       b. But wealth cannot buy life
       c. And was buried. A great funeral with hired mourners
       d. Listing his accomplishments
       e. Minister may have preached him right into glory
    4. It is appointed unto man once to die (Heb. 9:27)

C. THE CONTRAST OF THEIR EXPERIENCES IN ETERNITY (vv. 22–31)
    1. Lazarus was carried by the angels into Abraham's bosom
       a. Christians who die now do not go to Abraham's bosom
       b. That was only before Calvary
       c. Angels now carry Christians right to heaven
    2. The rich man awoke in hell
       a. The spirit equipped to see, hear, cry, speak
       b. The spirit can recognize . . . and remember
    3. The rich man's great concern about lost brothers
       a. His concern surpasses the concern of most Christians
       b. Send Lazarus. No, the Bible is enough

III. CONCLUSION
    A. NO MAN IS PREPARED TO LIVE UNTIL PREPARED TO DIE
    B. DO YOU CARE ABOUT THOSE WHO WILL DIE LOST?
    C. LAZARUS CANNOT GO AND TELL THEM! WILL YOU?

THE BIRTH OF A NATION

Hebrews 11:8–10; *Genesis* 12:1–3

I. INTRODUCTION
   A. THE THREE BEGINNINGS
      1. Genesis 1: Beginning with Adam
      2. Genesis 6—7: Beginning with Noah
      3. Genesis 12: Beginning with Abram
   B. WHEN THE WORLD REBELS, GOD DEALS WITH ONE MAN
      1. The Tower of Babel
      2. Out of the confusion comes a call
      3. God will give birth to the nation Israel through Abram
      4. Many lessons here for individuals and for any nation longing for God's blessings

II. BODY
   A. GOD CALLS ABRAM TO A LIFE OF FAITH (v. 1)
      1. "Get thee out of thy country"
         a. Ur of the Chaldees, Abram's country
         b. Great surprise to archeologists: an advanced civilization
      2. Abram, a wealthy man in Ur
      3. "Unto a land that I will show thee"
         a. Abram must leave the known for the unknown
         b. The first great adventurer in the Bible
         c. He must turn from the wealth that calls him to the Word that calls him
      4. Reminds us of the faith of the Pilgrims leaving Europe to settle in the New World
      5. Notice the proofs of Abram's faith
         a. He obeyed and went as God had commanded
         b. He refused to allow strife to grow among brethren (13:8–10)
         c. He tithed all he had (14:21)
         d. He refused rewards from the King of Sodom (14:22–23)

   B. GOD CALLS ABRAM TO A LIFE OF FRUITFULNESS (v. 2)
1. "I will make of thee a great nation"
   a. Compensation for leaving his country
   b. Abram's descendants today
2. "I will bless thee"
   a. Compensation for any earthly joy he might receive
   b. Only faith can thus be satisfied
3. "I will make thy name great"
   a. Compensation for leaving his kindred
   b. Name written down in heaven
   c. Consider Abram's name carried by millions and revered
4. "Thou shalt be a blessing"
   a. Compensation for putting aside opportunities of service
   b. Christ born in his line
5. We must also return to the faith of our fathers if we are to be blessed

   C. GOD CALLS ABRAM TO A LIFE OF DIVINE FRIENDSHIP (v. 3)
1. The friend of God
2. "I will bless him that blesseth thee and curse him that curseth thee"
3. No nation has ever been able to mistreat Abram's descendants and survive
4. God keeps Abram aware of His plan
5. "In thee shall all families of the earth be blessed"
   a. The coming Savior through the line of Abram
   b. We are all blessed through Abram
6. We become a blessing to others as we walk closely with God

III. CONCLUSION
   A. WILL YOU RESPOND IN FAITH LIKE ABRAM?
   B. WILL YOU BEGIN TO PRAY FOR A RETURN TO GOD IN AMERICA?
   C. WILL YOU BE AN EXAMPLE OF THE FAITH LIFE TO OTHERS?

FAITH: WHAT IT IS AND WHAT IT DOES!

Hebrews 11:1

I. INTRODUCTION
   A. AN IMPORTANT WORD IN THE BIBLE
      1. Ephesians 2:8–9: We are saved by faith in Christ
      2. Romans 5:1: We are justified by faith in Christ
   B. FAITH DEFINED
      1. The assurance of things hoped for
      2. The conviction of their reality
      3. Believing God to the point of action
      4. Humanity's favorable response to God's revelation
   C. HOW FAITH AFFECTS OUR LIVES

II. BODY
   A. FAITH MADE ABEL WORSHIP GOD (v. 4)
      1. We do not know many details of Abel's faith
         a. We do not know just how much was revealed to him
         b. Remember that Adam walked with God
      2. We do know that his faith caused him to worship God
         a. Picked the choicest lamb as an offering
         b. Brought it to the place of sacrifice
      3. Something wrong with the life that does not worship
      4. "Can't I be saved and stay away from church?"
         a. Something wrong with that faith experience
         b. Faith looks for opportunity to worship
   B. FAITH MADE ENOCH WALK WITH GOD (vv. 4–6)
      1. He walked with God (Gen. 5:22–24)
      2. How our walk will be changed if we trust in Christ (2 Cor. 5:17)
      3. He pleased God. Can that be said of your life?
         a. Is God pleased with the places you choose for recreation?
         b. Is God pleased with the books you read?
         c. Is God pleased with the words that you speak?
         d. Is God pleased with the plans you have for the future?
      4. His walk of faith delivered him from death

C. FAITH MADE NOAH WORK FOR GOD (v. 7)
   1. The tragic story of the decline of humanity into sin
       (Gen. 6)
   2. Grace triumphs: God will save Noah (v. 8)
   3. But if God will save, there must be real faith that
       produces works
       a. Noah will build an ark because he believes God
       b. Every swing of the hammer says, ''Faith''
       c. Every swing of the axe says, ''Faith''
       d. Every felled tree says, ''Faith''
       e. Every move of the brush as he applies the pitch
           says, ''Faith''
   4. So faith will make us work today
       a. Caring, sharing, witnessing
       b. Fishing for men

III. CONCLUSION
   A. HAS FAITH BEGUN IN YOUR LIFE?
   B. WHAT HAS FAITH CHANGED IN YOUR LIFE?
   C. WHERE ARE FAITH'S EVIDENCES IN YOUR LIFE?

MULTIPLIED BREAD

John 6:1–14

I. INTRODUCTION
    A. THE MIRACLE DESCRIBED BY ALL FOUR GOSPEL WRITERS
        1. The great discourse on the bread of life
        2. The lesson: "I am the bread of life"
    B. THREE PEOPLE MENTIONED IN CONNECTION WITH THE MIRACLE
        1. Phillip . . . Andrew . . . the boy who gave his lunch
        2. Lessons from their lives and words for us today

II. BODY
    A. PHILIP . . . WHO WAS FIGURING ON THE LEAST (vv. 5–7)
        1. "Whence shall we buy bread that these may eat?"
        2. We can identify with this problem
            a. This is a problem about daily bread
            b. Some are surprised that Christians have problems
        3. Note that Jesus saw the problem before Philip did
            a. Nothing takes Jesus by surprise
            b. The question to prove Philip
            c. Jesus knew what He would do all the time
        4. Philip . . . figuring on the least: "That every one of them may take a little"
            a. Many see only problems and focus on them
            b. Focusing on problems limits horizons
            c. He should have focused on the power of God
        5. Most of us live far below our potential
    B. ANDREW . . . WHO WAS FINDING FOR THE LORD (vv. 8, 9)
        1. Some are always fretting over problems, others are finding possibilities
        2. Andrew as a finder
            a. Right after coming to Jesus he found Peter (John 1:40, 41)
            b. Often those who are newly converted are best finders

        c. Do you remember when you were a finder?
     3. Andrew did not rule out any possiblity
        a. That lunch was a small thing . . . but he reported it
        b. Elijah needed only a cloud the size of a man's hand to expect rain (1 Kings 18)
        c. Whatever you have is enough for God
  C. THE LITTLE LAD WHO GAVE ALL HE HAD (vv. 10–14)
     1. The struggle that precedes surrender
     2. The unrecorded part of the miracle
        a. The struggle over the call to give his all
        b. The struggle that called for concern for others
        c. The struggle that called for faith: he was hungry
     3. The lunch given to Jesus . . . THE WIDE-EYED BOY
        a. The disciples distributing food
        b. The miracle, the satisfied people, the boy's joy

III. CONCLUSION
  A. YOU CANNOT LOSE WHEN GIVING ALL TO JESUS
  B. THE CALL TO FULL SURRENDER

WHAT DOEST THOU HERE?

1 Kings 19:1–15

I. INTRODUCTION
  A. ELIJAH, PROPHET OF GOD
    1. His rank . . . appeared with Jesus on the mount of Transfiguration
    2. One of the great prophets of the Old Testament
  B. AN ACCOUNT OF HIS LIFE
    1. Burst on the scene announcing a famine (1 Kings 17)
    2. Fed by the ravens and a widow; then came Carmel's great victory (1 Kings 17—18)
    3. Almost a shame to look in on him at this time, a time of defeat
    4. Here he is running for his life

II. BODY
  A. THE LORD'S CARE OF ELIJAH (vv. 4–8)
    1. Elijah's great victory and Jezebel's anger
    2. Now his victories are all forgotten . . . FEELS MIGHTY LOW
    3. A day's journey into the wilderness:
      a. Does not want to face anyone
      b. Does not want to talk to anyone
      c. Does not want to assume any responsibility
    4. Decides there is not any use in living
      a. It is enough . . . "I've had it!"
      b. Take my life away. Suicide is on his mind. HOW SAD!
    5. See how confused he is: He flees death yet seeks it!
    6. The depressed person does not know what he wants
    7. Finally flops down under a juniper tree and goes to sleep
      a. Have you ever felt so down that all you could do was lie down?
      b. Have you felt that life is fruitless and useless?
    8. But notice God's tender care of the depressed prophet
      a. As he slept, an angel touched him. God was watching

115

      b. Food and water provided, Elijah wakes and eats

      c. He sleeps and the angel wakes him again. Was not fed just to sleep

  B. THE LORD'S QUESTION TO ELIJAH (v. 9)

    1. "What doest thou here, Elijah?"

    2. God's question to His discouraged child

      a. Elijah was trembling when he should have been trusting

      b. Elijah was pouting when he should have been praising

    3. Here is God's question to a Christian defeated by fear

    4. Here is God's question to a Christian who thinks he has no purpose to live

    5. Here is God's question to a Christian who is over-whelmed by problems

    6. Here is God's question to one focusing on the faults of others

    7. Here is God's question to one who is backslidden

    8. Here is God's question to one who remembers a better day

  C. THE LORD'S COMMISSION TO ELIJAH (vv. 11-15)

    1. "Go forth and stand on the mount"

    2. What an experience he had!

      a. A great strong wind rent the mountains

      b. The ground trembles beneath his feet . . . stones fall

      c. Trees burst into flame . . . lightning strikes

    3. Why all this commotion if God is not in it? Had to get his attention!

    4. What must God do to get your attention?

    5. "What doest thou here?" Again!

    6. Elijah's answer . . . BUT SOMETHING HAPPENS BE-TWEEN (vv. 14, 15) that GET'S ELIJAH ON THE MOVE . . . HE IS COMMISSIONED: GO!

III. CONCLUSION

  A. GOD MEETS US WHERE WE ARE!

  B. HE COMMISSIONS US TO GET MOVING

  C. WHAT DOEST THOU HERE?

SEVEN THOUSAND SILENT SAINTS

1 Kings 19:18

I. INTRODUCTION
  A. ELIJAH: PROPHET OF POWER
    1. Could pray earnestly and prevent rain
    2. Could pray again and bring a cloudburst
    3. Fire from heaven . . . even the dead to life again
  B. ELIJAH'S EXPERIENCE OF DEFEAT AND DEPRESSION (1 Kings 19)
  C. THE SEVEN THOUSAND SILENT SAINTS
    1. Mentioned to cheer Elijah when he feels he is all alone
    2. Even God speaks little of them: here and Romans 11:4
    3. Quite a revelation to Elijah: He didn't know they existed
    4. What we know of this group
      a. They belonged to God
      b. They had not bowed the knee to Baal
      c. They had not kissed him
    5. Their testimony was entirely negative

II. BODY
  A. THE EFFECT OF THE SILENT SAINTS ON THE SERVANT OF GOD
    1. Discouraged, defeated, downhearted
    2. Hardly compares with his illustrious past
      a. His bravery in facing Ahab and Jezebel
      b. His faith in awaiting food from the ravens
      c. His stand against the compromising prophets
    3. But prophets and preachers are people
      a. Because given to deep feeling and spiritual peaks, they are often targets for depression
      b. Spurgeon and his times of feeling down. He preached a sermon titled "A Preacher's Fainting Fits."
      c. Nothing more worthless than a discouraged preacher
    4. The shameful pattern

117

        a. Studies show that preachers a bit older have not the same vision as when young

        b. Instead the vision should enlarge

B. THEIR EFFECT UPON THE FORCES OF EVIL

    1. No aggressive movement at all, only negative

    2. They were only known by the things they did not do

        a. Some Christians are like them

        b. Time for positive action

    3. The call for action

        a. Matthew 4:13–15: light of the world . . . salt of the earth

        b. Acts 1:8; Matthew 18:18–20: commissioned to serve

C. THEIR EFFECT ON EACH OTHER

    1. No evidence that anyone knew of the faith of the others

    2. Compare Acts 2 . . . 120 present . . . then 3000 . . . then 8000

    3. Each one keeping silent kept the others silent

    4. Our responsibility is to build up one another

III. CONCLUSION

A. LET THE WORLD KEEP SILENT

B. LET THE REDEEMED OF THE LORD SAY SO

MAN'S DEADLIEST WEAPON

James 3:1–10

I. INTRODUCTION
  A. THE BOOK OF JAMES . . . THE BOOK OF ACTION
    1. Faith is not something intangible that does nothing
    2. Faith without works is dead
    3. Faith that links with God and changes every part of life
  B. FAITH MUST ALSO HAVE ITS INFLUENCE OVER THE TONGUE
    1. This little member of the body rates an entire Bible chapter
    2. Dynamite comes in small packages

II. BODY
  A. THE TONGUE'S TREMENDOUS POWER IN RELATION TO ITS SIZE (vv. 1–5)
    1. Bits in horses mouths . . . rudders of ships
    2. Changes in the course of life
      a. "I do" in marriage
      b. "Guilty" in court
    3. The power of the tongue has changed the course of nations
      a. In 1896, William Jennings Bryan, an alternate delegate, became a candidate
      b. Patrick Henry's cry
    4. The tongue is like a fire . . . destructive:
        "The tongue can speak a word whose speed,
        Outstrips the very fastest steed"
  B. THE TERRIBLE PERIL OF THE TONGUE UNTAMED BY THE POWER OF GOD (vv. 6–8)
    1. "And the tongue is a fire, a world of iniquity"
    2. The tongue can defile the whole body (v. 6)
    3. The tongue is set on fire of hell
      a. Families torn apart by uncontrolled tongues
      b. Words spoken in anger between husbands and wives

           c. Harsh words spoken by Christians to one another

           d. Board meetings . . . congregational meetings . . . groups

      4. Full of deadly poison

           a. Critical tongues have closed church doors

           b. Never allow a negative or critical word to pass your lips

  C. THE THRILLING POSSIBILITIES OF A GOD-CONTROLLED TONGUE (v. 9)

      1. "Therewith bless we God"

      2. Romans 10:9: "Confess with thy mouth the Lord Jesus"

      3. Acts 1:8: "Witness unto me"

           a. The opportunity of witnessing

           b. The tongue's highest purpose

           c. Teaching a class

           d. Training our children in the way of the Lord

           e. Speaking a tender word to a troubled soul

           f. Speaking words to bring peace between enemies

           g. Telling friends and associates of God's love for them

      4. Psalms and hymns and spiritual songs (Eph. 5:19)

      5. Psalm 71:8: "Let my mouth be filled with thy praise"

III. CONCLUSION

  A. HOW GOD CHANGED THE TONGUES OF MEN

      1. Moses, stuttering then speaking to Pharoah

      2. Peter, cursing then preaching on Pentecost

      3. Paul, consenting to Stephen's death then TELLING THE GOOD NEWS

  B. SUBMIT YOUR TONGUE TO GOD

  C. SEE HOW MANY ARE HELPED.

        "Heaviness in the heart of a man maketh it stoop,
        But a good word maketh it glad" (Prov. 12:25)

TOUCH THE HEM OF HIS GARMENT

Luke 8:43–48

I. INTRODUCTION
   A. THE HEM OF HIS GARMENT
      1. Songs, poems, sermons on the hem of His garment
      2. This is the story behind that statement
   B. THE STORY OF A WOMAN IN GREAT TROUBLE
      1. Desperation, determination, deliverance, declaration
      2. Touch the hem of His garment

II. BODY
   A. A WOMAN'S DESPERATION (v. 43)
      1. The story of her problem all in one verse
         a. She had an incurable disease (sickness)
         b. She had spent all on the physicians
         c. She was ceremonially unclean
      2. Physically desperate, her health was gone
      3. Financially desperate, her money was gone
      4. Spiritually desperate, she could not enter the temple
      5. She is a picture of all people
         a. Physically, we are ever moving toward death
         b. Financially, money cannot buy what one needs
         c. Spiritually, sin separates us from God
   B. A WOMAN'S DETERMINATION (v. 44)
      1. "Came behind and touched the border of His garment."
      2. Things to discourage her from coming to Jesus
         a. The great crowd of people milling about Him
         b. The attitude of His disciples
         c. The importance of His mission
         d. Her own appearance: pale and poor
      3. Mark 5:28 gives the thoughts she had
      4. Still she pressed through to Jesus
   C. A WOMAN'S DELIVERANCE (vv. 45–46)
      1. Her deliverance came from contact with Jesus
      2. That touch of His garment was the touch of faith (v. 48)

121

       3. She exercised far greater faith than she thought she could
       4. She got more than she came for
          a. Her illness was healed
          b. She became a child of God: "Daughter, Go in peace!"

  D. A WOMAN'S DECLARATION (v. 47)
       1. "Who touched me?" Did Jesus know?
       2. Many surround Christ who do not touch Him
       3. Notice her simple testimony. She told why she had touched Him and how she was healed immediately
       4. Her testimony still heard today

III. CONCLUSION
  A. PRESS THROUGH TO JESUS
       1. The fear of what others will say
       2. What if this woman had not pressed through
  B. COME WITH YOUR NEED TO JESUS

GOD AT THE DOOR

Revelation 3:20

I. INTRODUCTION
   A. A FAMILIAR TEXT
      1. Taught in the Sunday School
      2. Familiar in its language: man knocking at a door
   B. THE SETTING AND THE SCENE
      1. John exiled on the Isle of Patmos
      2. Jesus' messages to the seven churches
      3. Then, "Behold!" Take notice
      4. Christ turns to the individual

II. BODY
   A. WHERE JESUS STANDS
      1. At the heart's door
      2. The humble place . . . difficult to find people to knock on doors
         a. Tough to get people to do door-to-door selling
         b. Visitation programs are a continual struggle
         c. Door-knocking can be a frightening experience
      3. How like Jesus to take the humble place
         a. Born in a stable . . . lived among men . . . crucified
         b. He understands your need
         c. The Gospel: Christ died for your sins, was buried, and rose again
      4. How strange that God should knock on your heart's door
      5. Do you recognize that He is there now?
   B. HOW JESUS KNOCKS
      1. He knocks with His hand
         a. The hand of God moves circumstances
         b. He's got the whole world in His hand
         c. The hand of God is setting the stage of prophetic fulfillment
         d. Nations and nature are moving according to plan
      2. He calls as He knocks

          a. "If any man hear my voice"
          b. He speaks through His Word, the Bible
          c. He speaks through His servants, ministers of the gospel
          d. He speaks through the lives of Christians
          e. He calls in love . . . and with urgency

  C. WHAT JESUS WILL DO IF YOU OPEN THE DOOR
     1. "I will come into him"
     2. The sure promise
        a. Our part is to open the door
        b. The Lord's part: "I will come in"
     3. How can Jesus come in?
        a. By His Spirit
        b. We become partakers of the nature of God (2 Peter 1:4)
        c. Your body becomes His temple (1 Cor. 6:19–20)

III. CONCLUSION
  A. DO YOU FEEL HIM KNOCKING?
  B. DO YOU HEAR HIS VOICE?
  C. WILL YOU OPEN THE DOOR?

GROW IN GRACE

2 *Peter* 3:18

I. INTRODUCTION
   A. THE CHRISTIAN LIFE BEGINS WITH A BIRTH
      1. Upon receiving Christ we are born again (John 1:12–13)
      2. Nicodemas and the new birth (John 3)
   B. THIS IS WHAT SEPARATES THE GOSPEL FROM RELIGION
      1. Religion is man's effort to reach up to God
      2. Salvation is God coming down to man and making him a new creation
   C. BUT AFTER BIRTH COMES GROWTH

II. BODY
   A. WHAT IS GROWTH IN GRACE?
      1. What it is not:
         a. It is not becoming more saved than at the moment of conversion
         b. It is not becoming more pardoned than when converted
         c. It is not becoming more justified than at salvation
      2. What Christian growth is: "When I speak of growth in grace I mean increase in the degree, size, strength, vigor and power of the graces which the Holy Spirit plants in a believer's heart" (J. C. Ryle)
      3. Consider the expectations of physical growth
         a. In a child, a flower, a tree
         b. The gardener and his garden
      4. Consider Bible evidences of growth in men
         a. Peter: From backsliding to blessing
         b. Paul: From the Damascus road to the Roman road
         c. John: From Son of Thunder to the disciple of love
   B. WHAT ARE THE EVIDENCES OF GROWTH?
      1. An increase of love (1 Thess. 3:12; 4:9–10)
         a. By this shall all men know that you are my disciples (John 13:35)

125

      b. How we know that we have passed from death to life (1 John 3:14)

      c. We are nothing without love (1 Cor. 13)

   2. An increase of faith (2 Thess. 1:3)

      a. What great promises attend this fruit of the Spirit!

      b. Most of us are but in the kindergarten of faith

   3. An increase of the knowledge of God (Col. 1:10)

      a. What you saw in Christ when you accepted Him compared to now

      b. Do you know more about God now than when you were saved?

   4. A greater desire for holiness in life (Phil. 3:13)

C. WHAT ARE THE MEANS THAT GOD USES TO HELP US GROW IN GRACE?

   1. He uses His Word (1 Peter 2:2)

      a. You never outgrow your need for milk

      b. There's a new you coming every day

      c. Look in the book first

   2. He uses trouble and experience (Rom. 5)

   3. He uses the private devotional life

   4. He uses public worship and service

   5. He uses the fellowship of believers

      a. How our needs are met by others (1 Cor. 12)

      b. What friendships and fellowships do to us

III. CONCLUSION

  A. ARE YOU GROWING?

  B. IF NOT . . . WHY NOT?

INDICATIONS OF INFANCY

I. INTRODUCTION
   A. THE NECESSITY OF THE NEW BIRTH
      1. Nicodemus and his search for eternal life
      2. Our Lord's startling revelation on the new birth
      3. Explaining the new birth to a religious man (John 3)
   B. GOD'S PLAN IS BIRTH, GROWTH, AND MATURITY
      1. We recognize this immediately in the physical realm
         a. This was even true of Christ
         b. We see it in our children. We expect growth and development. Vitamins . . . utmost care . . . trips to the doctor
      2. But spiritual growth is often neglected
         a. Much attention until conversion . . . then neglect
         b. Some remain infants for many years
      3. The Corinthian catastrophe: They had not grown
   C. HOW CAN WE RECOGNIZE SPIRITUAL INFANCY?

II. BODY
   A. THE SPIRITUAL INFANT IS CONCERNED WITH SELF RATHER THAN SERVICE
      1. The time of great rejoicing at birth . . . or salvation
         a. In heaven and here . . . snatched from the burning
         b. Delivered from destruction so all attention is on him
      2. Same is true with natural birth: all eyes on the baby
      3. Getting accustomed to attention
         a. Pampering the baby and the results
         b. Walking the floor night after night
      4. An infant is upset over the smallest things
         a. Some Christians have to be handled with kid gloves
         b. They wear their feelings on their sleeves
         c. They are like bombs . . . always ready to explode
            (1) At church extra nice, but at home explosive
            (2) At church she's ideal, but at home impossible
            (3) At church he's always praising, but at home pouting

(4) At church he's Mr. Good, but at home Mr. Grouch

(5) At church she's an example, but at home exasperating

5. The infant is a receiver . . . not a giver

a. The spiritual infant examines everything as a receiver

b. Fussing over rights

B. THE SPIRITUAL INFANT IS CONCERNED WITH ARGU-MENT RATHER THAN ACTION

1. Envying, strife, divisions are his occupation

2. Perhaps the most underestimated sin in our lives is strife

a. Galatians 5:19–21; Philippians 1:27; 2:1–4

b. Colossians 3:8–13; 1 Thessalonians 3:12; 2 Thessalonians 1:3–4

3. Have you ever watched children fight?

4. It is always easier to be part of the faction than to get into the action

5. Easier to grumble than to go, easier to argue than to act

C. THE SPIRITUAL INFANT LOOKS TO PEOPLE RATHER THAN TO THE MASTER

1. "I am of Paul . . ."

2. The infant's world: mother, father, baby sitter

3. If mother and father do not respond, he despairs and screams

4. The spiritual infant looks to human resources

a. The person who led him to Christ

b. The evangelist who preached a special sermon

c. Many miles to hear a singer, a preacher, a program . . . but can't get to an evening service or prayer meeting

III. CONCLUSION

A. WHAT DOES THE SPIRITUAL INFANT NEED?

1. To look to Christ

2. To begin building

3. To remember the judgment seat of Christ

B. ISN'T IT TIME TO GROW UP?

GUIDES FOR GROWTH

I. INTRODUCTION
  A. GROWTH IN PHYSICAL LIFE
    1. For babies, growth tells the story
    2. The tragedy of not growing
    3. Maturity is the goal
  B. THE CHRISTIAN LIFE
    1. Birth, growth, maturity
    2. Growth as revealed in songs
      a. "To Jesus every day I find my heart is closer drawn"
      b. "Every day with Jesus is sweeter than the day before"
      c. "Into the love of Jesus, deeper and deeper I go"
  C. GUIDES FOR GROWTH

II. BODY
  A. WHAT MUST I FORSAKE IF I AM TO BECOME A MATURE CHRISTIAN? (v. 1)
    1. There are certain cherished relics of childhood
      a. A little girl may have her favorite doll
      b. A little boy may have his favorite blanket or bear
    2. But it is natural for these to be put away in maturity
    3. "When I became a man I put away childish things" (1 Cor. 13:11)
    4. According to Paul . . . some childish things are envy, strife, divisions
    5. Peter agrees . . . put away:
      a. All malice, bitterness: wrong feelings toward another
      b. Guile . . . disposition to hypocrisy
      c. Hypocrisy . . . the act lived out
      d. Envy . . . is tormented with another's good
      e. All evil speakings . . . slanderings . . . gossip
  B. ON WHAT MUST I FEED IF I AM TO BECOME A MATURE CHRISTIAN? (v. 2)
    1. Proper food for proper growth

2. What are you feeding your mind? Your heart? Your soul?

3. We are affected by what we take in

4. Some things are detrimental to spiritual growth
   a. Much of today's reading material
   b. A high percentage of today's television
      (1) Profanity
      (2) Bedroom scenes
      (3) Unmarrieds living together promoted as natural
      (4) Drinking as a sign of the good life

5. But God's Word develops spiritual growth
   a. Desire . . . have an eager longing like a hungry baby
   b. Cultivate a hunger for the Bible as a baby hungers for milk

C. WHO MUST I FOLLOW IF I AM TO BECOME A MATURE CHRISTIAN? (v. 21)

1. Heroes a part of every childhood

2. Most of my boyhood heroes have toppled

3. A young Christian may idolize the person who led him to Christ, a certain musician or evangelist

4. Whom do you follow?

5. Keep your eyes on Jesus

III. CONCLUSION

A. ARE RELICS OF SPIRITUAL INFANCY HANGING ON?

B. HOW IS YOUR DEVOTIONAL LIFE?

C. LET'S GET GROWING!

MARKS OF MATURITY

Ephesians 4:7–16

I. INTRODUCTION
  A. WHAT MAKES CHRISTIANITY DIFFERENT?
      1. The Christian life begins with spiritual birth . . . not ceremony
      2. The new birth takes place when you receive Christ as Savior
  B. GOD'S PLAN: BIRTH, GROWTH, MATURITY
  C. INDICATIONS OF INFANCY
      1. More concerned with self than service
      2. More concerned with argument than action
      3. Looking to man rather than to God
  D. HOW CAN WE RECOGNIZE CHRISTIAN MATURITY?

II. BODY
  A. THE MATURE CHRISTIAN IS A BELIEVER WITH A MISSION (vv. 11–12)
      1. Perfecting means maturing
      2. The gifts of the Lord to the church are to bring us to maturity
          a. The apostles and prophets through their writings
          b. Evangelists through their special ministry
          c. Pastors and teachers have the primary responsibility in bringing about Christian growth
      3. Now we see the mistake in understanding the pastoral role
          a. The pastor has become the one who does the work of the ministry instead of maturing others to do it
          b. Instead of being participants, Christians have become spectators
          c. Pastors perform and their people go home to talk about it
          d. Too many believers feel their responsibilities end in paying pastors and supporting missionaries
      4. Mature believers see their mission in life as doing the work of the ministry: reaching out to others with the love and gospel of their Savior

B. THE MATURE CHRISTIAN IS A BUILDER OF OTHER BELIEVERS (v. 12)
1. "For the edifying of the body of Christ"
2. "Edify" means to build up or help along
    a. Christ is the head of the church
    b. Each believer is a member
3. What can you do to build up the body of Christ?
    a. You can care for parts of the body that are afflicted
        (1) Prayer for the sick
        (2) Visiting the fatherless and widows (James 1:27)
    b. You can care for the physical needs of the body
        (1) Paul and the offerings for the saints in Jerusalem
        (2) Too long we have left this to social agencies
    c. You can help care for the spiritual needs of the body
        (1) Be a peacemaker
        (2) Live and teach the Scriptures
4. Are others stronger in Christ because of you?
5. Is the body more unified because of you?
C. THE MATURE CHRISTIAN HAS A BIBLE BASIS FOR EVERY BELIEF (v. 14)
1. "No more children, tossed to and fro"
2. No longer snared or attracted by cultic teachings
3. Solid in doctrine
4. Do you know why you believe what you believe?
5. Maturity in the Word of God brings maturity in life

III. CONCLUSION
A. EXAMINE YOURSELF FOR THE MARKS OF MATURITY
B. IN WHAT AREAS ARE YOUR GREATEST NEEDS FOR GROWTH?
C. LET'S AID ONE ANOTHER ON THE ROAD TO CHRISTIAN MATURITY

SOME NEGATIVES IN THE MATURE CHRISTIAN

SERIES ON GROWTH   *Ephesians* 4:17–32

I. INTRODUCTION
   A. THE DELIGHTFUL PROSPECT OF GROWING UP
      1. Both children and parents are pleased at growth
         a. The first smile or tooth
         b. The first steps and words
      2. The Christian life also has such progress
      3. After the new birth, growth is natural
   B. WE MATURE SO THAT WE CAN TAKE RESPONSIBILITIES WHICH BRING SATISFACTION
      1. This is a principle of life
      2. Irresponsibility sounds like freedom but ends in emptiness
      3. Accomplishments bring satisfaction
      4. In this maturing process, some negatives are necessary
   C. WHAT ARE THE NEGATIVES OF CHRISTIAN MATURITY?

II. BODY
   A. WALK NOT AS OTHER GENTILES WALK (vv. 17–25)
      1. There is to be a difference (2 Cor. 5:17–18)
      2. This is really saying: "Walk not as you used to walk" (Eph. 2:1–8)
         a. According to the course of this world
         b. According to the prince of the power of the air, Satan
         c. According to the lusts of the flesh
         d. Fulfilling the desires of the flesh and the mind
      3. How does the world walk?
         a. In the vanity of the mind
         b. Having their understanding darkened
         c. Having blind hearts
         d. Giving themselves to lasciviousness
         e. Working uncleanness with greediness
   B. LET NOT THE SUN GO DOWN UPON YOUR WRATH (v. 26)

      1. Never let a day end being angry
      2. Some people live with anger constantly
         a. Anger gets things for them and moves others
         b. Tantrums unless they get their way
         c. Sulking, sobbing, silence
      3. We are never to let a day end with anger
         a. Some sad situations between husbands and wives
         b. Thunder and lightning each night
      4. How shall we deal with anger? Give it to Jesus . . . confess and forsake

C. LET HIM THAT STOLE STEAL NO MORE (v. 28)
      1. How strange a statement like this is necessary
      2. Some addicted to stealing
         a. Shoplifting, taking things from employers
         b. Stealing from others
         c. Stealing from God (Mal. 3:10)
      3. The call to generosity and honesty

D. LET NO CORRUPT COMMUNICATION PROCEED OUT OF YOUR MOUTH (v. 29)
      1. By our words we are to be judged
      2. James and his comments about the tongue
      3. What is corrupt communication? Some get as close to profanity as possible
      4. Psalm 19:14: "Let the words of my mouth . . ."

E. GRIEVE NOT THE HOLY SPIRIT OF GOD (v. 30)
      1. Your body His temple
      2. This should make you careful . . . help you mature
      3. Stop grieving the Lord in word, thought, or deed

III. CONCLUSION

A. WHAT SHALL WE DO IF THESE THINGS REMAIN IN OUR LIVES?
      1. Confess them as sin (1 John 1:9)
      2. Present our bodies to Christ as living sacrifices (Rom. 12:1)

B. GROW UP!

POSITIVES IN THE CHRISTIAN LIFE

Ephesians 4:17–32

I. INTRODUCTION
  A. NEGATIVES IN THE MATURE CHRISTIAN LIFE
     1. Walk not as other Gentiles
     2. Let not the sun go down upon your wrath
     3. Let him that stole steal no more
     4. Let no corrupt communication proceed out of your mouth
     5. Grieve not the Holy Spirit of God
  B. HAS THE HOLY SPIRIT USED THESE IN YOUR LIFE?
  C. THEN LET US GLEAN SOME POSITIVES FROM THE SAME TEXT

II. BODY
  A. BE RENEWED IN THE SPIRIT OF YOUR MIND (v. 23)
     1. Notice the preceding verse
        a. We are to put off the old man
        b. Throw out the works of the flesh (Gal. 5:19–21)
     2. The Christian may neglect his mind
        a. If he does, he may act like a lost person
        b. But he is urged not to do so
     3. The danger of neglecting proper mind input and reaction
        a. The downward road (Rom. 1:18–32)
        b. This can be avoided by renewing the mind (Rom. 12:1–2)
     4. Our minds need renewing every day
  B. PUT ON THE NEW MAN (v. 24)
     1. The Christian is a paradox
        a. He has the potential for failure
        b. He has the old nature that never improves as long as he lives
     2. He also has the Holy Spirit residing in him
        a. This places unlimited power at his disposal for victory

      b. He has actually become a partaker of divine nature

      c. Christ is able to live through his body (Gal. 2:20)

    3. He has the power that raised Christ from the dead

    4. Talk about the six million dollar man!

    5. He has all that he needs for victorious living

C. LABOR SO THAT YOU CAN GIVE TO THOSE IN NEED (v. 28)

    1. Here is a unique purpose for working

    2. Why do you work?

      a. To make a living?

      b. To prepare for retirement?

      c. To leave a fortune for your children?

      d. To make investments?

    3. Here is a better reason: To give to those in need

    4. It is more blessed to give than to receive

D. BE KIND ONE TO ANOTHER (v. 32)

    1. If you are not very kind, you are not very spiritual

    2. Kindness that results in being tender to the needs of others

    3. Kindness that makes it easy to forgive

    4. Kindness that demonstrates the love of Christ to others

III. CONCLUSION

    A. DIFFERENT . . . MATURE . . . READY FOR RESPONSIBILITY

    B. EFFECTIVE IN CHRISTIAN SERVICE AS THE LORD LIVES THROUGH US

LEARNING TO WALK

I. INTRODUCTION
   A. CHRISTIAN GROWTH MAY NOT MATTER TO YOU
      1. If you have not been born again
      2. If you are content with mere formal Christianity
      3. If you are backslidden and in a spiritual rut
   B. BUT CHRISTIAN GROWTH IS NORMAL FOR BELIEVERS
      1. Growth naturally follows birth
      2. Evidences of growth should be seen in all of us continually
   C. LEARNING TO WALK

II. BODY
   A. WALK IN LOVE (v. 2)
      1. Why not mentioned as the first sign of growth?
         a. The gospel is the greatest love story
         b. Only saved after realizing God's love for us
      2. Perhaps because this has to do with passing love on to others
      3. Others are to be recipients of our love (God's love through us)
      4. This love is proof of genuine faith
         a. Proof of discipleship (John 13:35)
         b. Proof of new life (1 John 3:14)
         c. Proof of the Holy Spirit within (1 Peter 1:22)
      5. How this affects disposition and conduct
         a. Greater concern for others
         b. Greater kindness in speaking and acting
         c. Greater compassion for those in trouble
         d. The example of Jesus
   B. WALK AS CHILDREN OF LIGHT (v. 8)
      1. This command reaches from verse 3 to verse 14
      2. Light and darkness in the Bible
         a. Light speaks of God and righteousness
         b. Darkness speaks of Satan and all evil

        c. See Romans 13:11–14
    3. Note how darkness is set forth in the text
        a. Fornication, uncleanness, covetousness (v. 3)
        b. Filthiness, foolish talking, jesting (v. 4)
        c. Whoremongers, unclean persons, covetous person, idolater (v. 5)
    4. In contrast, note how light is described
        a. Goodness, righteousness, truth (v. 9)
        b. What is acceptable unto the Lord (v. 10)
        c. Rejecting and reproving the works of darkness (v. 11)
    5. Christ is the source of light (v. 14)
  C. WALK CIRCUMSPECTLY (v. 15)
    1. "Looking around"
    2. Walking with our eyes open and alert to what is going on
    3. The person who walks circumspectly:
        a. Has his eyes open to the needs of others
        b. Has his eyes open to the will of God
        c. Has his eyes open to the signs of the times
    4. The circumspect walk is one that seizes opportunities
        a. Realizes the time is short
        b. Realizes the seriousness of the situation
III. CONCLUSION
  A. HOW'S YOUR WALK?
  B. THE CALL TO PROPER WALKING:
    1. In love
    2. In light
    3. Looking around

THE GROWING CHRISTIAN AND HIS ENEMY

Series on Growth   *Ephesians* 6:10

I. INTRODUCTION
   A. NOW YOU'RE ON THE GROW
      1. Some have made new commitments to Christ
      2. Some have rebuilt altars once broken down
      3. Devotional life for some has been revived
      4. The marks of maturity are starting to show up
   B. SOMEONE DOESN'T LIKE IT
      1. You have an enemy who frowns on your spiritual progress
      2. His purpose is to hinder you on your road to higher ground

II. BODY
   A. THE ADVERSARY (vv. 10-18)
      1. The text reveals a determined enemy
         a. Be strong
         b. Put on the whole armor of God
         c. Wrestling
      2. The reality of Satan's existence
         a. The Bible speaks of him again and again
         b. His purpose is your destruction (John 10:10)
         c. He often operates as an angel of light (2 Cor. 11:14)
         d. He goes about the earth as a roaring lion (2 Peter 5:8)
         e. He will someday have a political representative (Rev. 13)
      3. There is a spiritual battle raging constantly
      4. Every Christian has enlisted to oppose the enemy
   B. THE ASSOCIATES IN THIS BATTLE (v. 10)
      1. "Finally, my brethren" (Eph. 6:10)
      2. You are not in this battle alone
         a. Others have to face the same foe
         b. At salvation, you are born into this fighting fellowship

    c. Let us be sure that we fight the foe . . . not each other

  3. Let us learn to help in this battle with the adversary
    a. Is another Christian struggling with temptation?
    b. Is a brother or sister discouraged?
    c. Is a fellow Christian passing through difficulty?
  4. You are a pilgrim . . . but not the only pilgrim
  5. Rush to the aid of those in the conflict
    a. Quickly to your knees in prayer
    b. Words of encouragement to those in need

C. THE AVAILABLE RESOURCES IN THIS BATTLE (v. 10)
  1. "Be strong"
    a. You may feel weak
    b. But you can draw on God's strength
  2. "Be strong in the Lord and in the power of His might"
  3. The power of the Holy Spirit within each believer
  4. The power of prayer available to all
  5. The power of the Word of God
  6. The power of the blood of Christ
  7. The power of a conquering Savior

III. CONCLUSION
  A. BORN TO WIN
  B. YOU DO NOT HAVE TO BE DEFEATED
  C. MAKE USE OF YOUR RESOURCES AND KEEP GROWING

THE GROWING CHRISTIAN AND HIS BATTLE WITH THE ENEMY
Part I

          Ephesians 6:10–18

I. INTRODUCTION
  A. THE CHRISTIAN LIFE IS ONE OF CONSTANT CONFLICT
    1. This is discouraging to some
    2. Had hoped to move on to heaven with ease
    3. We are locked in conflict with the world, the flesh, and the devil
    4. A spiritual battle is raging all through the believer's life
      a. The struggle with Satan
      b. The battle against demonic powers
  B. THIS CONFLICT CAN BE ONE OF VICTORY AFTER VICTORY
    1. The victory of Christ at the cross
    2. We are equipped to win

II. BODY
  A. THE GIRDLE OF TRUTH
    1. Satan called the father of lies (John 8:44)
    2. The girdle of truth to oppose him
      a. The girdle to keep flowing robes from tangling
      b. Israel on the first Passover night (Exod. 12:11)
      c. Dishonesty trips us up
      d. No one has a good enough memory to be a successful liar
    3. Truthful about ourselves in dealing with sin (1 John 1:7–9)
    4. Truthful with God (Ps. 51:9)
    5. Truthful with others
  B. THE BREASTPLATE OF RIGHTEOUSNESS
    1. We are not saved by our righteousness
    2. Once converted, it is God's purpose to produce His righteousness in us
    3. The righteousness of Christ is ours through faith

       4. His righteousness showing through us
       5. Both of these are needed
         a. I need to have Christ's righteousness
         b. Others need to see Christ's righteousness in me
       6. This is both positional and practical
       7. Do right! And right things will follow
       8. We cannot do wrong and expect spiritual victory
  C. THE PREPARATION OF THE GOSPEL OF PEACE
       1. What is the gospel?
       2. When did you hear it first?
       3. The preparation of the gospel of peace: being able to share the gospel with others
       4. Why it is called the gospel of peace (Rom. 5:1)
       5. Feet shod with the gospel of peace: moving out to others with the gospel
       6. The best defense is a good offense
       7. As long as we are standing still, we are easy targets
       8. Take the gospel to others and experience victory

III. CONCLUSION
  A. TRUTH, RIGHTEOUSNESS, SOUL WINNING
  B. WHAT PART DO THESE PLAY IN YOUR DAILY BATTLE?
  C. GET THEM IN PLACE AND BEGIN TO WIN

THE GROWING CHRISTIAN AND HIS BATTLE WITH THE ENEMY
Part II

SERIES ON GROWTH   *Ephesians* 6:16–20

I. INTRODUCTION
   A. THE ENEMY . . . THE ARMOR . . . THE ENERGY
      1. The enemy: The prince of the power of the air (Satan) and demons
      2. The armor (vv. 14–16)
      3. The energy (v. 18)
   B. HALF-DRESSED FOR THE BATTLE
      1. The girdle of truth
      2. The breastplate of righteousness
      3. The preparation of the gospel of peace
   C. THE REST OF THE ARMOR

II. BODY
   A. THE SHIELD OF FAITH (v. 16)
      1. Two things strike us immediately
         a. We are under attack by fiery darts
         b. Faith is the most important part of the armor (above all)
      2. Two types of shields used in that day
         a. A large shield to hide behind (*thereos*)
         b. A small shield to move about (*aspis*)
         c. It is the large one indicated here
      3. Satan sends fiery darts
      4. The shield of faith is so effective it will quench them *all*
         a. Faith can overcome every attack of the enemy
         b. Darts of pride, envy, worry, fear, lust
      5. The power of faith. See Hebrews 11
   B. THE HELMET OF SALVATION (v. 17)
      1. We know this has to do with the head
         a. The home of the mind
         b. A "know-so" salvation

      2. The assurance of salvation enables us to stand against the enemy

      3. Consider Paul's assurance:

         a. Speaking boldly (v. 20)

         b. "I know whom I have believed" (2 Tim. 1:12)

      4. Moody: "I never knew a person who was effective in the Lord's service who did not have assurance of his salvation"

  C. THE SWORD OF THE SPIRIT (v. 17)

      1. The sword of the Spirit is the Word of God

      2. The one offensive weapon in the armor

      3. The weapon Jesus used against Satan in the temptation (Matthew 4)

      4. To be used to conflict with the devil

      5. David's weapon for keeping a clean life (Ps. 119:9–11)

      6. We never know the impact of even one text

      7. The power of God's Word over the enemy

III. CONCLUSION

  A. SUMMARY OF ALL THE ARMOR

  B. PRAYING ALWAYS (v. 18)

      1. Prayer is the communication line from headquarters

      2. Prayer is needed for victory

  C. ONWARD CHRISTIAN SOLDIERS

THE CITY GOD WANTED TO SAVE

I. INTRODUCTION
   A. AN IMPORTANT BOOK IN THE OLD TESTAMENT
      1. The story of Jonah: called to preach and finally swallowed by the great fish
      2. Used as a type of the death and resurrection of Christ
      3. The entire account authenticated by Jesus
   B. AN EXTREMELY FITTING BOOK TO STUDY IN THE LIGHT OF WORLD CONDITIONS

II. BODY
   A. THE CALL OF GOD TO SAVE A CITY (vv. 1, 2)
      1. God calls His servant and there is a good reason
      2. The countdown has begun for a great city! Six weeks left
         a. The countdown of wickedness
         b. The countdown of life
         c. The countdown of prophetic fulfillment
      3. Is there any hope? YES!
      4. But that hope rests in a prophet named Jonah, and he is relaxing
         a. "Jonah, arise." Get moving
         b. Jonah stands for the sleeping church in this crucial hour
         c. Nineveh stands for a lost world tottering on the brink of doom and destruction
   B. THE CONDITION OF JONAH'S HEART (v. 3)
      1. Rebellious and disobedient
         a. "Go to Nineveh." He went to Joppa
         b. Told to go east and went west
      2. Do you know a point of departing from God's will?
      3. The downward trail of backsliding
         a. It is always so
         b. Either higher ground or downward bound
      4. God had more trouble getting His servant going than He did in getting Nineveh to repent

    C. THE CHASTENING OF JONAH (vv. 4–16)
   1. The Lord chastens His children (Heb. 12:4–11)
   2. The storm: God pursues His own
   3. Jonah asleep in the storm
   4. God's purpose in our trials
   5. The sailors' reaction
   6. Their searching question: "Why hast thou done this?" (Jonah 1:10)

    D. THE CATCHING OF JONAH BY THE GREAT FISH (vv. 11–17)
   1. Jonah's instruction and calming of the sea (vv. 11–15)
   2. The prayers of the sailors (v. 16)
   3. The miracle of the great fish (GOD WOULD GO TO ANY LENGTH TO GET JONAH RIGHT BECAUSE HE HAD A JOB FOR HIM TO DO)

III. CONCLUSION
    A. THE COUNTDOWN CONTINUES
    B. WHAT IS THE CONDITON OF YOUR HEART
    C. JONAH BROUGHT TO THE PLACE OF PRAYER
    D. WHAT MUST GOD BRING INTO YOUR LIFE TO BRING YOU TO HIMSELF AND HIS WILL?

JONAH'S PRAYER

I. INTRODUCTION
   A. THE CITY GOD WANTED TO SAVE . . . NINEVEH
      1. Located on the East bank of the Tigres River
      2. Covered a large area
         a. 60 miles around
         b. Population of 600,000
   B. GOD CALLS A MAN TO DELIVER THE MESSAGE
      1. Jonah, a prophet according to Jesus
      2. Jonah flees
         a. More trouble getting his servant willing than in bringing Nineveh to repentance
         b. Down to Joppa, down into the ship, down into the sides of the ship
         c. The storm, the sailors, the great fish
   C. JONAH'S PRAYER

II. BODY
   A. WHERE HE PRAYED!!! (vv. 1, 2)
      1. "Out of the fish's belly"
         a. A strange place to pray
         b. Not a place one would choose
         c. It was where he was and that was the place to pray
      2. "And He heard me"
      3. Two great lessons here:
         a. God hears us anywhere
         b. Far better to pray in normal surroundings than to wait until we are in abnormal surroundings
      4. Now is the accepted time
   B. WHY HE PRAYED!!! (v. 2)
      1. "By reason of my affliction"
      2. Hadn't been praying for some time
         a. Fleeing from God
         b. Neglecting his spiritual responsibilities
         c. Sleeping during the storm . . . chastening

      3. He really was afflicted:
         a. "Out of the belly of hell cried I" (v. 2)
         b. "Cast into the deep" (v. 3)
         c. "The floods compassed me about" (v. 3)
         d. "Thy billows and waves passed over me" (v. 3)
         e. "The waters compassed me about, even to the soul" (v. 5)
         f. "The weeds were wrapped about my head" (v. 5)
  C. WHEN HE PRAYED!!! (v. 7)
      1. When his soul fainted within him
      2. Jonah was now at the end of himself
         a. No more running
         b. No more spiritual deafness
         c. Like the prodigal son
      3. Jonah's change of heart
         a. "I remembered the Lord"
         b. "I will sacrifice unto thee"
         c. "I will pay that I vowed"
         d. "Salvation is of the Lord"

III. CONCLUSION
  A. GOD'S DELIVERANCE OF JONAH
      1. Jonah on dry ground
      2. Delivered from trouble
  B. THE WORD OF THE LORD CAME THE SECOND TIME TO JONAH
      1. God's call is renewed
      2. It is not too late to be used of God

THE SECOND TIME

I. INTRODUCTION
   A. THE CITY GOD WANTED TO SAVE . . . NINEVEH
      1. A great and wicked city
      2. A city that was in the countdown to judgment
         a. The countdown of wickedness, of life, of prophetic fulfillment
         b. Six weeks until destruction
   B. JONAH . . . THE RELUCTANT PROPHET
      1. Called, chosen, but flees
      2. Swallowed by the great fish: A type of death, burial, resurrection
   C. THE WORD OF THE LORD CAME THE SECOND TIME

II. BODY
   A. THE SECOND CALL CAME AFTER FAILURE AND CHASTENING (chaps. 1, 2)
      1. So many things about Jonah's response to God's call were wrong
         a. His attitude was wrong. He knew better than that
         b. His fleeing. He knew better than that
         c. Choosing self will. He knew better than that
      2. Chastening comes to the wayward child of God
      3. Christians can never get away with sin (Heb. 12:4–11)
         a. That storm was no accident
         b. The great fish was no accident
      4. Examples of those under God's chastening
         a. Israel wandering in the wilderness for forty years
         b. Samson grinding in the prison house: blind and powerless
      5. But God's grace reaches those who have failed
         a. Samson would return and regain his strength
         b. Peter, even though he wept because of his denials, became the spokesman of the church
         c. And God will meet you where you are

149

B. THE SECOND CALL CAME WITH JONAH'S OLD COM-
MISSION (3:2)
1. This second call is evidence of God's wonderful grace
2. Jonah must have thought it was all over for him
   a. Rising there on the beach: exhausted and done in
   b. Thought deliverance was the best that could
      happen
   c. Probably doubted that God would ever use him
      again
3. But God called Jonah the second time with the same
   message
4. The God of the second chance: not for salvation, but
   service
5. The blessed message of Psalm 51
C. THE SECOND CALL CAME IN SPITE OF THE FACT THAT
JONAH WOULD FAIL AGAIN (chap. 4)
1. Jonah was displeased with Nineveh's repentance
2. Here is a man who is disappointed with his own success
3. Here is a preacher who regrets that God has used him
4. Here is an evangelist who is pouting over a whole city of
   penitents
5. What hard hearts we have! *Still God loves us*

III. CONCLUSION
A. WHATEVER YOUR PAST, GOD WILL MEET YOU TODAY!
B. EVEN IF YOU ARE TO BE WEAK AND FAIL TOMORROW,
HE WILL MEET YOU TODAY
"No physician ever weighed out medicine to his patients
with half so much care and exactness as God weighs out to
us every trial. Not one grain too much does He ever permit
to be put in the scale." (Henry Ward Beecher)

THE REVIVAL IN NINEVEH

I. INTRODUCTION
   A. THE ROAD TO NINEVEH
      1. The call of God and the fleeing of Jonah
      2. The great fish and Jonah's second chance
      3. Finally, the great revival
   B. DO WE NEED A REVIVAL IN AMERICA TODAY?
      1. We probably have no idea just how much!
      2. We are also in the countdown
      3. Zero hour may be upon us
   C. THE INGREDIENTS IN THE REVIVAL IN NINEVEH

II. BODY
   A. THE PREACHING OF JONAH (vv. 3–5)
      1. Jonah approaches the great city
         a. 60 miles around it, 600,000 people
         b. Walls 100 ft. high, three chariots abreast
         c. No advance men, no radio, no television, no P.A. systems
      2. Wickedness in the city . . . people preoccupied with sinful pursuits
      3. Jonah was an earnest preacher. His experience was fresh
         a. A message of coming judgment
         b. A message of limited opportunity: forty days
         c. Plain . . . powerful . . . personal
      4. Jonah knew that God was in earnest, and so was he!
      5. Jonah's faith was contagious
   B. THE PENITENCE OF THE KING (vv. 6, 7)
      1. The people believed God
      2. But now this reaches to the king
      3. How hard it is for the privileged to be penitent!
         a. The rich young ruler
         b. Felix, "A more convenient season" (Acts 24:25)
         c. Agrippa, "Almost thou persuadest me to be a Christian" (Acts 26:28)

   4. Repentance is unusual to the rich and powerful
   5. The king's discovery:
      a. Riches were not enough, he needed righteousness
      b. Power was not enough, he needed peace
      c. Servants were not enough, he needed salvation
   6. The king's penitence moved the whole city to repentance
C. THE PRAYERS OF THE PEOPLE (vv. 8–10)
   1. "Cry mightily unto God"
   2. 2 Chronicles 7:14: "If my people"
   3. From a straying people to a praying people
   4. From committing sin to confessing sin
   5. The ingredient without which no revival has ever come
   6. What their crying did:
      a. Caused the city to be spared
      b. Delivered them from destruction

III. CONCLUSION
   A. NINEVEH SHALL RISE IN JUDGMENT (Matt. 12:38–41)
   B. APPLICATION AND CALL TO PERSONAL REVIVAL

THE POUTING PROPHET

I. INTRODUCTION
   A. A BRIEF INTERLUDE IN JONAH'S LIFE
      1. We know nothing about his past . . . before his call
      2. We know nothing about him after completion of his mission except the brief narrative given in chapter 4
   B. JONAH POUTING AFTER NINEVEH REPENTS
      1. Learning more about Jonah
      2. His reaction to success

II. BODY
   A. HIS LACK OF LOVE FOR NINEVEH (vv. 1–3)
      1. Now we know why he had rebelled at God's call
      2. He didn't like the Ninevites because they were not Jews
      3. How easy it is to fall into sectarianism: Color, race, etc
      4. But all have sinned and come short of the glory of God (Rom. 3:23)
      5. There is no difference
      6. The cross demonstrates God's love for all people
         a. The ground is level at the foot of the cross
         b. All need to be saved and all can be saved
      7. We must not close our minds to the needs of people
   B. HIS LOVE OF PLEASURE (v. 5)
      1. Building his booth at the east side of the city
      2. Waiting for God's judgment to fall on Nineveh
         a. Wondering why God's judgment does not fall
         b. But think of God's grace that keeps us from His judgment
      3. The Lord will not let Jonah get away with this attitude
         a. The gourd that grows up overnight
         b. The worm that causes the gourd to die
         c. The east wind blowing on Jonah's bald head
      4. To Jonah . . . pleasure was more important than people
      5. Comfort was more important than saving a city
      6. There are many like him

   C. HIS LOVE OF SELF (v. 9)
      1. How easy to fall into this trap!
      2. Self-pity is one of the respectable sins
      3. One of the sins that brings us to despair and depression
      4. Justifying the sin of anger: "I do well to be angry"

III. CONCLUSION
   A. GOD PLEADING WITH THE POUTING PROPHET
      1. Lessons from the gourd
      2. Comparison of people to plants
   B. THE CHAPTER ENDS WITH GOD STILL PLEADING
   C. HEAR GOD PLEADING WITH YOU
      1. Do you care about people?
      2. What has priority in your life?
      3. Does self rule or the Savior?

REVIVAL

I. INTRODUCTION
  A. REVIVAL, A MISUNDERSTOOD WORD
     1. Used often but often used wrongly
     2. More than a series of meetings
  B. WHAT IS REVIVAL?
     1. Revival is specifically the business of Christians
     2. It has to do with bringing back life
     3. Walter Boldt: "Revival is God at work, restoring His church to health." That is an acceptable definition if we understand that a healthy church is a soul-winning church. Revival must result in reaping
     4. Revival can be the experience of the whole body of Christ, a local church, or of one Christian
  C. IMPORTANT FACTS ABOUT REVIVAL

II. BODY
  A. IT IS RIGHT TO PRAY FOR REVIVAL
     1. "Wilt thou not revive us again?"
        a. The psalmist is praying for revival
        b. All revivals begin in prayer
     2. Moody: "Every great work of God can be traced to a kneeling figure"
     3. "If my people, which are called by my name, shall humble themselves and pray" (2 Chron. 7:14)
     4. "When they had prayed, the place was shaken" (Acts 4:31)
     5. What are you doing about prayer for revival?
        a. Extra time in prayer?
        b. Extra prayer meetings?
  B. IT IS RIGHT TO EXPECT REVIVAL
     1. "Wilt thou not revive us again?"
     2. Most believe revival has taken place in the past
        a. They believe wicked Nineveh repented
        b. They believe the early church turned the world upside down

      c. They believe John and Charles Wesley brought revival to England

      d. They believe Jonathan Edwards saw revival in colonial America

      e. They believe Charles Finney and A.C. Lanphier were used to bring the revival of 1857

      f. They thrill to stories of the Welsh revival

   3. But they do not believe God will bring revival today

   4. Sometimes this is a result of a misunderstanding of prophecy

   5. Sometimes it is an unwillingness to pay the price of revival

   6. There will always be defeatist voices

   7. But God is unchanged!

   8. We can have revival now!

  C. IT IS RIGHT TO EXPECT REJOICING TO RESULT FROM REVIVAL

   1. Revival may begin in tears, but it proceeds to joy

   2. The Christian who is continually grieving over past sins does not understand the grace of God and needs revival

   3. Revival and rejoicing go hand in hand

      a. The coal mines in Wales were filled with singing

      b. The taverns were empty, the courts without cases some days

      c. Revival finds God's people focusing on Jesus, resulting in joy

III. CONCLUSION

  A. HOW REVIVALS START: WITH A FEW CONCERNED PEOPLE

  B. ARE YOU WILLING TO LET REVIVAL BEGIN IN YOU?

REVIVAL . . . IN SUCH A TIME

I. INTRODUCTION
   A. AMERICA IS IN NEED OF A GREAT REVIVAL
      1. There has never been a more serious hour
      2. The troubled world, the moral slide, the countdown
      3. It is time for a genuine revival . . . must start in the churches
   B. ISAIAH THE PROPHET LIVED IN SUCH A TIME
      1. See chapter one: a wayward people
      2. See chapter five: woes pronounced
      3. See chapter six: Isaiah revived in such a time
   C. OUR NEEDS AND ISAIAH'S TRANSFORMING VISION

II. BODY
   A. A NEW AWARENESS OF THE CHARACTER OF GOD (vv. 1–4)
      1. In the year that King Uzziah died (v. 1)
         a. Uzziah, a great and powerful king
         b. When he died, Isaiah saw the Lord
      2. Isaiah, now unable to look to Uzziah, looks to God and finds out what God is really like
      3. What is God like?
         a. He is all powerful . . . omnipotent
         b. He is all knowing . . . omniscient
         c. He is everywhere . . . omnipresent
         d. He is eternal
      4. Isaiah had to learn that He is holy
         a. Holy, holy, holy . . . the trinity
         b. Moses, take the shoes off your feet . . . holy ground (Exod. 3:5)
         c. The cross, the supreme example of God's holiness
      5. God has not changed (Rev. 4:8)
   B. A NEW AWAKENING OF CHRISTIAN CONSCIENCE (vv. 5, 6)
      1. "Then said I . . . Woe is me!" Contrast to preceding chapter of woes

2. Isaiah saw himself measured by God's standard
3. Last days . . . consciences seared with hot iron (1 Tim. 4:2)
   a. Old fashioned honesty hard to find
   b. Rubber band convictions
4. Hear Isaiah's confession
   a. "I am undone"
   b. "I am a man of unclean lips"
   c. "I live in the midst of a people of unclean lips"
5. Note how specific he is
6. Note also the wonderful, clear message of forgiveness (v. 6)

C. A NEW CONCERN FOR THE SOULS OF MEN (v. 8)
1. The Lord's question: "Whom shall I send?"
2. Isaiah's response, "Send me"
3. People will pray almost anything else
4. But revival produces soul winners, people who care
5. Are you willing to go wherever the Lord sends or leads?

III. CONCLUSION
A. THE LORD'S QUESTION STILL SOUNDS
B. WHAT WILL YOUR ANSWER BE?
C. WHEN YOUR HEART IS RIGHT, YOU ARE READY TO SERVE

THE PRISON REVIVAL

I. INTRODUCTION
  A. REVIVALS AND RIOTS
     1. Wherever Paul went he had either a revival or a riot
     2. Strange that his revivals were sometimes in prison and his riots in the temple . . . but maybe not so strange
     3. In this text he had both
  B. REVIVAL AT AN UNUSUAL TIME
     1. Revivals have characteristically come at unusual times and places
     2. The blessings of a revived church
  C. INGREDIENTS IN THE PRISON REVIVAL

II. BODY
  A. TWO CHRISTIANS IN REAL PRAYER (v. 25)
     1. Paul and Silas prayed
        a. No wonder they prayed
        b. Blessed is the affliction that drives us to our knees
        c. But these men prayed before trouble came (v. 16)
     2. When they prayed . . . at midnight
        a. This may seem to be your darkest hour
        b. But it is never too dark to pray
        c. Our God delights to work in the dark
     3. Prayer is always the foundation of revival
        a. Moody: "Every great work of God can be traced to a kneeling figure"
        b. Calling churches to prayer . . . you may be the key
     4. How they prayed: specifically, believingly
  B. TWO CHRISTIANS WITH THE RIGHT ATTITUDE (v. 25)
     1. ". . . and sang praises"
     2. The praying is not strange. The praising is the miracle
        a. Reasons they might have been depressed:
           (1) They had obeyed the Macedonian call (v. 9)
           (2) They had been winning souls (vv. 14, 15)
           (3) They had been prayerful (v. 16)

159

(4) They had been sensitive to the need of the demon-possessed woman and released her (vv. 16–18)
   b. Still trouble had come
   3. Nevertheless they praised God!
      a. Focused on God's power instead of their problems
      b. Believed that God would deliver them
      c. Identified with Jesus, the stocks, the darkness, stripes
   4. The value of PRAISE!!!
C. TWO CHRISTIANS IN THE RIGHT PLACE (v. 28)
   1. The earthquake, freedom, opportunity to escape
   2. The jailor's fears, Paul's surprising statement
   3. Christians in the right place
      a. In relation to the church, all of the services
      b. In relation to the world, separation
      c. In relation to the Lord, abiding in Him
D. TWO CHRISTIANS WITH THE RIGHT MESSAGE (v. 31)
   1. The greatest question: "What must I do to be saved?"
   2. The only answer: "Believe on the Lord Jesus Christ . . ."

III. CONCLUSION
   A. THE CONVERSION OF THE JAILOR
   B. THE IMPACT OF THE PRISON REVIVAL
   C. WHAT WOULD A GENUINE REVIVAL CHANGE ABOUT YOUR LIFE?

THE REVIVAL WE NEED

I. INTRODUCTION
   A. In light of the times, we need a revival
   B. DEFINITIONS OF REVIVAL
      1. Walter Boldt: "God at work restoring His church to health"
      2. Finney: "Return to the first love resulting in conversion of sinners"
   C. WHAT KIND OF A REVIVAL DO WE NEED TODAY?

II. BODY
   A. REVIVAL THAT RESURRECTS THE CHURCHES
      1. Revival means a return of life
         a. The return of life is resurrection
         b. The example of Lazarus, dead four days
         c. New life to a church
      2. A spiritual resurrection that is like the physical resurrection that will take place when Jesus comes
         a. A revival that awakens the saints . . . the trumpet sound
         b. A revival that gets the saints on the move
         c. A revival that brings new vision
         d. A revival that makes the world take notice
      3. What would happen if revival came to your church?
         a. What do you long for at this church?
         b. Are you willing to take the first step to make it happen?
   B. A REVIVAL THAT REKINDLES OLD FIRES
      1. Revive us *again* . . . must have been revived before
      2. The Christian life is made up of many beginnings
      3. Do you remember better days?
         a. Days of dedication
         b. Days of great expectations
         c. Days of full commitment
      4. Paul's word to the Galatians: "Ye did run well" (Gal. 5:7)

     5. Return to your Bethel . . . your greatest hour
        a. The day you were saved
        b. The time of your surrender to Christ
   C. A REVIVAL THAT REBUILDS BROKEN FELLOWSHIP
     1. . . . that *thy people* . . .
     2. Our walk with God is individual . . . but not isolated
     3. We need one another
        a. "Blest be the tie that binds our hearts in Christian love"
        b. Need to share, to care, to walk together again
     4. Consider the fellowship of the New Testament church (Acts 2, 4)
     5. The importance of looking beyond our borders
   D. A REVIVAL THAT RESTORES CHRISTIAN JOY
     1. So many defeated Christians!
     2. So many cranky Christians!
     3. So many discouraged Christians!
     4. So many backslidden Christians!
     5. The joy of the Lord is your strength (Neh. 8:10)
     6. May God give you a song again

III. CONCLUSION
   A. THE CALL TO PERSONAL REVIVAL
   B. MOST CAN LIVE ON HIGHER GROUND

WHY CHRISTIANS DON'T HAVE REVIVAL

I. INTRODUCTION
   A. TALKING ABOUT REVIVAL
      1. "God at work restoring His church to health," Walter Boldt
      2. "Never losing the wonder of it all," Gypsy Smith
      3. "Returning to that first love," Charles Finney
   B. DROUGHT AND THE STATE OF THE CHURCHES
      1. The drought of Israel
      2. Dry weather and the symbolic picture of the churches
      3. Water as a symbol of revival . . . refreshing
         a. "I stretch forth my hands unto thee: my soul thirsteth after thee as a thirsty land" (Ps. 144:6)
         b. "As the hart panteth after the water brooks, so panteth my soul after God" (Ps. 42:1)
         c. "He that believeth on me, as the scripture hath said, out of his belly shall flow rivers of living water" (John 7:38)
   C. REFRESHING RAIN AND WHY IT IS NOT FALLING MORE OFTEN, REGULARLY

II. BODY
   A. CHRISTIANS DO NOT HAVE REVIVAL BECAUSE THEY DO NOT PRAY FOR IT
      1. They pray, but often without feeling
      2. They pray, but often without faith
      3. They pray, but often their prayers are very formal
      4. They pray to keep the church going, but few pray specifically for revival
      5. Faith-filled revival praying brings revival
   B. CHRISTIANS DO NOT HAVE REVIVAL BECAUSE THEY DO NOT EXPECT IT
      1. "Go up now and look toward the sea"
      2. Elijah fully expected rain
      3. He sent his servant to look for it
      4. What are you looking for in the church?

      5. The servant returns having found nothing
      6. "Go again seven times." The blessing of expectation
      7. Let us expect the blessing of God. Let us expect revival
  C. CHRISTIANS DO NOT HAVE REVIVAL BECAUSE THEY DO NOT RECOGNIZE IT
      1. A cloud the size of a man's hand
      2. Elijah only needed a small sign to see the blessing
      3. Are you seeing revival?
      4. Do you recognize it?
      5. Is there evidence of God at work in your heart?

III. CONCLUSION
  A. RAISED EXPECTATIONS
  B. A CLOUD THE SIZE OF A MAN'S HAND
  C. LOOK FOR SIGNS OF REVIVAL
  D. FAN REVIVAL INTO FLAME

COMMUNION AND REVIVAL

I. INTRODUCTION
   A. HOW FITTING . . . REVIVAL AND COMMUNION
      1. Every communion ought to bring revival
      2. Calling us back to our first love
      3. A time for new dedication
   B. WHAT THE LORD'S TABLE IS NOT
      1. It is not a means to salvation
      2. It is not the table of this church alone
   C. WHAT IS COMMUNION?

II. BODY
   A. COMMUNION IS A TIME FOR LOOKING BACKWARD (vv. 23–25)
      1. Looking back to the cross
      2. The cross is our message (1 Cor. 1:18)
         a. Other messages are temporal
         b. But the message of the cross lasts
      3. Remembering the time it became personal
      4. What does Christ's death mean to you?
   B. COMMUNION IS A TIME FOR LOOKING INWARD (vv. 27–32)
      1. The case at Corinth
         a. Taking communion lightly
         b. Some sick and some had died
      2. A heart-searching time
      3. How to avoid chastening (v. 31)
      4. Time for breaking down barriers
   C. COMMUNION IS A TIME TO LOOK OUTWARD
      1. Communion is evangelistic
      2. The call to sinners to see the gospel in the symbols of Christ's death
      3. After the cross came commissioning (Acts 1)
      4. Every communion should send us out to reach the lost

    D. COMMUNION IS A TIME FOR LOOKING UPWARD (v. 26)
        1. ''Till he come''
        2. Jesus is coming
        3. The great reunion in heaven
III. CONCLUSION
    A. TIME FOR EXPRESSION
    B. FELLOWSHIP IN THE FAMILY OF GOD
    C. HOW WILL THIS COMMUNION CHANGE YOUR LIFE?

LIVING WATER

I. INTRODUCTION
   A. THE FEAST OF PENTECOST
      1. The great feast day, the Feast of Firstfruits
      2. The very day on which the Holy Spirit would later be given
      3. Here Jesus would make an announcement about the Holy Spirit
   B. REACTIONS ABOUT JESUS BY PEOPLE AT THE FEAST
      1. John 7:15, "How knoweth this man letters?"
      2. John 7:31, "When Christ cometh, will he do more miracles?"
      3. John 7:46, "Never man spake like this man"
      4. John 7:48, "Have any of the rulers or Pharisees believed on Him?"
   C. THE GREAT STATEMENT OF JESUS ABOUT THE HOLY SPIRIT

II. BODY
   A. THE INVITATION TO THOSE DESIRING THE HOLY SPIRIT (v. 37)
      1. "If any man thirst"
      2. Notice to whom the invitation is given
         a. Not to those who have prayed and fasted long enough
         b. Not to those who have prayed through . . . or loud enough
         c. Not to those who have repeated phrases of praises enough
         d. Not to those who have recently taken the sacraments
      3. But to those who are thirsty
      4. How wonderful to express it this way!
         a. Some here might not know how to get religious enough
         b. Some might not be able to reform enough

167

   c. Some might not understand theology enough

  5. But everyone knows how it feels to be thirsty

   a. Do you thirst to know that the guilt is gone?

   b. Do you thirst to know that the record is clean?

   c. Do you thirst for fellowship with God?

B. THE INSTRUCTION FOR RECEIVING THE HOLY SPIRIT

  1. "Let him come unto me and drink"

  2. To receive this refreshing water, come to Jesus and drink

  3. Consider the call by Isaiah (Isaiah 55:1)

  4. Consider the last invitation in the Bible (Rev. 22:17)

  5. What is meant by "come unto me and drink"?

   a. To come to Him is to believe on Him

   b. To come to Him is to trust Him

   c. To come to Him is to receive Him

  6. Note that the requirement for receiving the Holy Spirit is the same as that for receiving Christ

  7. Upon receiving Christ, the Holy Spirit comes into the believer

C. THE INNER FOUNTAIN THAT FLOWS WITHIN THOSE WHO HAVE RECEIVED CHRIST

  1. "Out of his innermost being shall flow rivers of living water"

  2. We are not to be cisterns but rivers

   a. Not like the Dead Sea . . . but a great river

   b. Not like a swamp . . . but a refreshing stream

  3. What will flow in these rivers?

   a. The fruit of the Spirit will flow in these rivers

   b. The compassion of Christ will flow in these rivers

   c. Power to witness will flow in these rivers

   d. Faith will flow in these rivers

III. CONCLUSION

 A. DO YOU THIRST?

 B. WILL YOU COME TO CHRIST AND DRINK?

THE HOLY SPIRIT: WHO HE IS AND WHAT HE DOES

SERIES ON THE HOLY SPIRIT   John 14:16, 17, 26; John 16:7–15

I. INTRODUCTION
  A. WHO IS THE HOLY SPIRIT?
    1. He is God
      a. As the Father is God
      b. As the Son is God
    2. The third person of the Trinity
  B. THE HOLY SPIRIT IS A PERSON
    1. The mistake of thinking of Him impersonally
      a. Some falsely teach He is only a force
      b. The Holy Spirit has intellect (Rom. 8:27)
      c. The Holy Spirit has emotion (Eph. 4:30)
      d. The Holy Spirit has a will (1 Cor. 12:11)
    2. These are the characteristics of personality
  C. BUT WHAT DOES THE HOLY SPIRIT DO?

II. BODY
  A. THE HOLY SPIRIT COMFORTS
    1. He is called the Comforter (John 14:16, 26; 16:7)
      a. How interesting that this is the first title used by Jesus
      b. How often we need comfort!
    2. We need comfort when separation is near
      a. Jesus was about to be separated from His disciples
      b. The cross and all its agony was ahead
    3. We need comfort when tears are near (Gethsemane)
    4. We need comfort when we feel alone
    5. We need comfort when others turn against us
    6. We need comfort when death has touched those near us
  B. THE HOLY SPIRIT COUNSELS
    1. "He shall teach you all things" (John 14:26)
    2. We need a counsellor when we are perplexed
      a. Many things in this troubled world perplex us

        b. Perhaps you are troubled and perplexed today
     3. Jesus had been a Counsellor to His disciples
     4. Now He would send the Holy Spirit to teach them
     5. The Holy Spirit is a Tutor
         a. Teaches us individually
         b. Teaches us continually
     6. What does He teach?
         a. All about the Bible (2 Peter 1:20–21)
         b. All about life (John 14:26)
         c. All about Jesus (John 14:26; 16:13–15)
  C. THE HOLY SPIRIT CONVICTS
     1. "He will reprove" (John 16:8–11)
     2. He convicts of sin
         a. People have consciences
         b. The Holy Spirit prods the conscience about sin
         c. Do you feel guilty? This is the Spirit's first work
            (1) Conviction comes before conversion
            (2) Correction comes before comfort
     3. He convicts of the lack of righteousness
         a. We have failed to do right
         b. Christ demonstrated a perfect life
         c. We fall far short of this perfect standard
         d. We are all sinners (Rom. 3:23)
     4. He convicts of judgment
         a. After death the judgment (Heb. 9:27)
         b. Prepare to meet God (Amos 4:12)
     5. The purpose of conviction is to bring us to Christ
III. CONCLUSION
  A. WHAT IS THE HOLY SPIRIT SAYING TO YOU TODAY?
  B. RESPOND TO HIS CONVICTION
  C. RECEIVE HIS COMFORT AND COUNSEL

RECAPTURING PENTECOST

SERIES ON THE HOLY SPIRIT   Acts 2:41–42

I. INTRODUCTION
  A. ANY STUDY OF THE HOLY SPIRIT WOULD HAVE TO INCLUDE PENTECOST
    1. The day of the coming of the Holy Spirit
    2. The birthday of the church
      a. The true church of the Lord Jesus
      b. The church that Christ is building
  B. WHAT WAS PENTECOST?
    1. It was not the beginning of a denomination
    2. It was so named because it was the fiftieth day after Passover
    3. The world did not know what had been happening during that time
      a. Christ had risen and had appeared to His disciples
      b. The disciples had been commissioned and witnessed the ascension
      c. The ten days of waiting and praying
  C. THE WORK OF THE HOLY SPIRIT ON THE DAY OF PENTECOST

II. BODY
  A. THE WORK OF THE HOLY SPIRIT IN CONVERSION (v. 41)
    1. "They that gladly received his word"
    2. Who gladly received His word?
      a. Three thousand who had come for the feast
      b. Three thousand who had been of the Christ-rejecting crowd
      c. No one is too far gone for the Holy Spirit to reach
    3. What was this word they gladly received?
      a. It was a message of conviction (v. 22)
      b. It was a message of the cross (v. 23)
      c. It was a message of the resurrection (v. 24)
    4. All real conversion is the work of the Holy Spirit
      a. The case of Nicodemus (John 3:1–8)

      b. The testimony of Paul to Titus (Titus 3:5)

  B. THE WORK OF THE HOLY SPIRIT IN PUBLIC WITNESS (v. 41)

     1. "Were baptized"

     2. Salvation takes place in the heart, but we confess Him openly

     3. Baptism is a public witness . . . identification with Christ

        a. The Holy Spirit and baptism . . . the dove

        b. The Holy Spirit moving you to this act of obedience

     4. Think of the hostile atmosphere at that time

     5. So much confusion on the subject

     6. Best to take the Bible literally

     7. You are in good company when you choose baptism

        a. Jesus chose it

        b. Paul chose it

        c. The converts on Pentecost chose it

     8. The Holy Spirit gives public expression to the Gospel through us

  C. THE WORK OF THE HOLY SPIRIT IN CHRISTIAN GROWTH (v. 42)

     1. "They continued . . ."

     2. They were not content to just escape hell . . . nor should we be

     3. The promise of the Holy Spirit to teach (John 14:16–18, 26)

     4. In fellowship: the bond between believers

     5. In breaking of bread . . . communion

     6. In prayers: the part the Holy Spirit plays in praying

     7. He leads us on to higher ground

III. CONCLUSION

  A. THE WORK OF THE HOLY SPIRIT IN YOUR HEART

  B. HOW WILL YOU RESPOND TO HIS MINISTRY?

THE HOLY SPIRIT AND CONVERSION

Titus 3:5; 1 *Corinthians* 6:19–20;
Ephesians 4:30; 1 *Corinthians* 12:13

I. INTRODUCTION
   A. THE WORK OF THE HOLY SPIRIT IN THE WORLD (John 16:8–14)
      1. Convicting of sin, righteousness, and judgment
      2. Teaching people about Christ and glorifying Him
      3. Bringing people to conversion
   B. WHAT THE HOLY SPIRIT DOES AT THE MOMENT OF SAVING FAITH

II. BODY
   A. THE HOLY SPIRIT BRINGS NEW LIFE TO THE BELIEVER (Titus 3:5)
      1. All are spiritually dead because of sin (Eph. 2:1–9)
      2. Nicodemus and Jesus (John 3)
         a. Nicodemus was religious but lost
         b. He needed a spiritual birth
         c. Apart from the new birth, he would not be saved
      3. Regeneration means new birth
         a. Most have yearned to be able to start life over again
         b. In the sight of God, you can do just that
   B. THE HOLY SPIRIT TAKES UP HIS RESIDENCE IN THE BELIEVER (1 Cor. 6:19–20)
      1. Dr. Kenneth Wuest: "The Holy Spirit takes up His permanent residence in us"
      2. Jesus promised this to His disciples (John 14:16–23)
      3. When the Holy Spirit comes in, there is evidence of the Occupant in the believer's life
         a. The Bible becomes a new book
         b. The fruit of the Spirit starts showing up in life
         c. Power to overcome sin becomes a daily experience
         d. A new longing for holy living becomes part of life

C. THE HOLY SPIRIT SEALS THE BELIEVER (Eph. 4:30)
1. Note the thrilling progression: REGENERATION, RESI-
DENCE, SEALING
2. Sealing speaks of ownership
a. The title of your car
b. Your marriage license
3. The presence of the Holy Spirit within the believer is
like a downpayment (Eph. 1:13–14)
4. To guarantee this sealing, we have the witness of the
Spirit (Rom. 8:14–16)
5. The sealing of the Spirit guarantees that what God has
begun He will continue to completion (Eph. 4:30)
D. THE HOLY SPIRIT BAPTIZES THE BELIEVER (1 Cor.
12:13)
1. Important to note that this takes place at conversion
2. The following facts must be noted about the baptism of
the Spirit
a. All references to the baptism of the Spirit before
Pentecost are prophetic
b. All references to the baptism of the Spirit after
Pentecost speak of it as something that happened
in the believer's life at conversion
c. No Scripture teaches us to seek the baptism of the
Spirit
3. The baptism of the Spirit places the believer into the
body of Christ
a. A new bond of fellowship
b. Now part of the family of God

III. CONCLUSION
A. NEW LIFE, INDWELT, SEALED, BAPTIZED: ALL AT
CONVERSION
B. IN VIEW OF THESE BENEFITS IN CHRIST, LET US WALK
IN THE SPIRIT
C. WE ARE EQUIPPED TO WIN

YOUR BODY, HIS TEMPLE

I. INTRODUCTION
- A. THIS IS A BODY-CONSCIOUS WORLD
  1. Many products to clean up, paint up, and fix-up
  2. Great concern about physical shape
     - a. Diets abound
     - b. Exercise clubs, etc
- B. THE CHRISTIAN HAS ANOTHER DIMENSION TO THIS ATTITUDE
  1. The day you became a Christian, something happened to your body
  2. That is the topic of this message

II. BODY
- A. YOUR BODY IS THE TEMPLE OF THE HOLY SPIRIT
  1. "What know ye not that your body is the temple of the Holy Ghost?"
  2. This reminds us of the temple in the Old Testament
     - a. What great care was given to its design
     - b. What immense wealth was placed into its construction
     - c. The people were to know that God dwelt there
  3. Note the day of dedication of Solomon's temple (2 Chron. 7:1–3 and 12–15)
  4. But there is no such place in the age of grace
     - a. This building is not God's temple
     - b. This building is not even a church, just the place the church meets
  5. Your body, God's temple:
     - a. Be careful where it goes
     - b. Be careful what it does
     - c. Be careful what it ponders
     - d. Be careful how it reacts
- B. THE HOLY SPIRIT LIVES WITHIN HIS TEMPLE
  1. "Who is in you"
  2. How can that be?

        a. Something like the creation of man

        b. Another proof of the mystery of God

    3. See how clearly the Bible bears out this truth

        a. Jesus makes the promise (John 14:15–26)

        b. The Book of Acts describes it (Acts 2:1–4; 4:31)

        c. The epistles explain it (Rom. 8:5–17; Gal. 3:1–5; Eph. 5:18–25)

    4. The result: THE HOLY SPIRIT IS WITH YOU WHEREVER YOU GO

        a. His power is available when you need it

        b. Every word and deed is in His view

        c. He is grieved at our inconsistencies

  C. THE PURPOSE OF THE HOLY SPIRIT IS TO GLORIFY GOD IN HIS TEMPLE

    1. The purpose of the creation of man

    2. Stephen glorifying God in giving his life

    3. Paul glorifying God in beatings and stonings

    4. John on the Isle of Patmos suffering for his Lord

    5. God can receive glory through your body and spirit

III. CONCLUSION

  A. SURRENDER YOUR BODY TO THE LORD

  B. GLORIFY GOD IN DAILY LIFE

THE HOLY SPIRIT AND
THE CHRISTIAN LIFE

SERIES ON THE HOLY SPIRIT   *Galatians* 3:1–6; 5:17–23

I. INTRODUCTION
  A. SOME THINGS WE HAVE LEARNED ABOUT THE HOLY SPIRIT
    1. That the Holy Spirit is a person having intellect, emotion, and a will
    2. That the Holy Spirit is the third person of the Trinity
  B. THE HOLY SPIRIT AND CONVERSION
    1. Regenerates the believer . . . brings new life (Titus 3:5)
    2. Takes up His residence in the believer (1 Cor. 6:19–20)
    3. Seals the believer (Eph. 4:30)
    4. Baptizes the believer into the body of Christ (1 Cor. 12:13)
  C. HOW CAN I KNOW WHETHER OR NOT THE HOLY SPIRIT IS WITHIN ME?

II. BODY
  A. THE PRESENCE OF THE HOLY SPIRIT PRODUCES FAITH (3:1–9)
    1. The Christian life begins with faith
      a. Paul had been to Galatia and many had believed
      b. There had been evidence of their new life
    2. The Holy Spirit will draw you to faith in Christ
    3. Now these converts had concluded that keeping the law was necessary
      a. Here is a mistake of many cults
      b. The law is fulfilled in Christ
    4. The Holy Spirit comes in response to faith, and He matures our faith
      a. He increases our faith through the written Word
        (1) He was at work in revelation (2 Peter 1:21)
        (2) He was at work in inspiration (2 Tim. 3:16)
        (3) He is at work in illumination (John 14:26)
      b. He increases our faith by revealing Christ, the living Word

        (1) This is the promise of our Lord (John 16:13–14)

        (2) The more we know of Jesus, the stronger our faith

B. THE PRESENCE OF THE HOLY SPIRIT PRODUCES A FIGHT (Gal. 5:17)

   1. Peace at the moment of conversion

     a. Spiritual life has come

     b. Fellowship with God becomes a reality

   2. But soon we learn we are in a war (1 Tim. 6:12; 2 Tim. 4:7)

     a. War with the devil (Eph. 6:11–12)

     b. War with the flesh (1 Cor. 9:27)

   3. What is the point of conflict?

     a. The Holy Spirit vs. the sin nature (Gal. 5:17–21)

     b. Consider Paul (Rom. 7:15–25)

   4. How do we stay victorious in this battle?

     a. By feeding the new nature on the Word of God

     c. By yielding to the Holy Spirit

C. THE PRESENCE OF THE HOLY SPIRIT PRODUCES FRUIT (Gal. 5:22–23)

   1. How to see who is winning the battle

   2. Here are the things the Holy Spirit wants to produce in you

   3. Notice the natural divisions in this list:

     a. First in relation to God . . . love, joy, peace

     b. Second in relation to fellowman . . . longsuffering, gentleness, goodness

     c. Third, in relation to ourselves . . . faith, meekness, self-control

   4. What a beautiful cluster of graces!

III. CONCLUSION

A. WHAT IS THE HOLY SPIRIT PRODUCING IN YOU?

B. BY YIELDING TO HIM, WE BECOME FRUITFUL

THE HOLY SPIRIT IN THE CHURCH

Acts 4:31

I. INTRODUCTION
   A. SAD THOUGHTS ABOUT JESUS AND THE HOLY SPIRIT
      1. Jesus was in the world and the world was made by Him and the world knew Him not
      2. The Holy Spirit was in the church and the church was made by Him and the church knew Him not
   B. WHAT ABOUT THE HOLY SPIRIT AND THE CHURCH?
      1. What if individual members were each filled with the Holy Spirit?
      2. What does the Holy Spirit want to do for and in us?
   C. EXAMPLES FROM THE EARLY CHURCH

II. BODY
   A. IN THE CHURCH, THE HOLY SPIRIT MAKES WITNESSES OUT OF WEAKLINGS (Acts 1:8)
      1. The death and resurrection of Christ
      2. Ascension Day and its questions
         a. Will the kingdom be restored today?
         b. Shall we start carrying out the Great Commission today?
      3. Witnesses after the Holy Spirit comes
         a. This witnessing to be done in divine power
         b. The word then was wait, then witness. Now it is witness immediately in the power of the Holy Spirit
      4. Consider the weakness of the disciples
         a. Peter and his denying of the Lord
         b. Philip and his weak faith
         c. Thomas and his inability to believe in the resurrection
      5. This tiny group turned the world upside down
   B. IN THE CHURCH, THE HOLY SPIRIT BRINGS FELLOW-SHIP INSTEAD OF FACTIONS (Acts 4:32)
      1. The possibilities of divisions among the disciples
         a. Peter's denials

        b. Thomas and his lack of belief

        c. They all forsook the Lord and fled at the crucifixion

    2. Now they are of one heart and of one soul

    3. Their bond is more important than their possessions

    4. Some churches where the Holy Spirit is named are divided

    5. It is always the work of the Holy Spirit to bring unity among members in the local church so outreach is unhindered

  C. IN THE CHURCH, THE HOLY SPIRIT PRODUCES GROWTH WITHOUT GIMMICKRY (Acts 4:33)

    1. Every instance of the Holy Spirit's power at work in the church brought growth

        a. Acts 2:41: 3,000 converts

        b. Acts 4:4: 5,000 converts

        c. Acts 5:14: multitudes of converts

        d. Acts 6:7: numbers multiplied

    2. There are ways to increase numbers with gifts and gimmicks

        a. Used often in churches

        b. Used often to bring in money to media ministers

    3. The use of gimmicks shows the lack of power

    4. Aren't you tired of gimmicks?

    5. Let's depend on the Holy Spirit

III. CONCLUSION

  A. WILL WE BE A SPIRIT-FILLED CHURCH?

  B. WILL YOU DO YOUR PART?

BE FILLED WITH THE SPIRIT

I. INTRODUCTION
   A. WHAT IS THE FILLING OF THE HOLY SPIRIT?
      1. To be filled with the Spirit is to be controlled by the Spirit
      2. The Holy Spirit comes into the believer at new birth
      3. When one is filled, he gives the Holy Spirit complete control
   B. WHAT HAPPENS WHEN ONE IS FILLED WITH THE SPIRIT?
      1. Church and family life are affected (Eph. 5)
      2. The fruit of the Spirit is evident in his/her life (Gal. 5:21–22)
      3. He/she becomes bold in witnessing (Acts 4:31, 33)
      4. Great generosity toward those in need (Acts 4:32)
   C. HOW TO BE FILLED WITH THE HOLY SPIRIT

II. BODY
   A. GRIEVE NOT THE SPIRIT (Eph. 4:30)
      1. You must stop grieving the Holy Spirit
      2. God can be grieved
         a. Moses wrote that God was grieved before the flood (Gen. 6:6)
         b. David wrote that God was grieved with grumbling Israelites (Ps. 95:10)
         c. Isaiah prophesied that Jesus would be acquainted with grief (Isa. 53:3)
         d. Jesus wept over wayward Jerusalem and at a grave (Luke 19:41; John 11:35)
      3. The wrong advice: "Don't go anywhere you can't take the Lord along."
         a. Christians cannot leave their Lord behind
         b. But they may grieve Him . . . break His heart
      4. What is it that grieves the heart of God? (See v. 31)
         a. You cannot be filled with bitterness and be filled with the Spirit

        b. You cannot be filled with anger and be filled with the Spirit

        c. You cannot be filled with malice and be filled with the Spirit

        d. You cannot be filled with hatred and be filled with the Spirit

    5. Confess these sins and forsake them . . . GRIEVE NOT THE SPIRIT

  B. QUENCH NOT THE SPIRIT (1 Thess. 5:19)

    1. You must stop quenching the Spirit

    2. To quench the Spirit is to stifle or suppress His work in you

    3. To quench the Spirit is to halt His work in your heart

    4. To quench the Spirit is to resist Him

    5. To quench the Spirit is to exalt your will above the will of God

    6. To quench the Spirit is to tune Him out

        a. Tuning to channel worry

        b. Tuning to channel fear

        c. Tuning to channel entertainment

        d. Tuning to channel greed

    7. When you stop quenching the Spirit, wonderful things will happen

        a. Doors will open

        b. You will have peace of mind

        c. You will then experience the work of the COMFORTER

  C. WALK IN THE SPIRIT (Gal. 5:16)

    1. You must start walking in the Spirit

    2. Walking speaks of faith

        a. The lame man arose and walked

        b. Peter walked on the water

    3. To walk in the Spirit is to take by faith that God has granted His filling and proceed accordingly

III. CONCLUSION

  A. SOME THINGS TO CONFESS: GRIEVING . . . QUENCHING

  B. ONE THING TO TAKE BY FAITH: HIS FILLING

  C. VERY PERSONAL: SOMETHING TO SETTLE ALONE

THE SPIRIT-FILLED PERSON

Ephesians 5:18—6:9

I. INTRODUCTION
  A. HOW TO BE FILLED WITH THE HOLY SPIRIT
    1. Stop grieving the Holy Spirit
    2. Stop quenching the Holy Spirit
    3. Start walking in the Spirit
  B. BUT WHAT ABOUT THE CHANGES THIS MAKES IN DAILY LIFE?
    1. How can we recognize a Spirit-filled person?
    2. What areas of life are affected by walking in the Spirit?

II. BODY
  A. THE SPIRIT-FILLED PERSON AND HIS WORSHIP (vv. 19–21)
    1. Back to the comparison: "Be not drunk with wine" ·
      a. The man who is drunk is not under his own control
      b. He staggers, he slurs his speech, he aims his car
    2. Like this: "Be under the control of the Holy Spirit"
    3. This makes all of life an experience in worship
      a. Worship in the heart
      b. Creates an attitude of praise
    4. But this does not mean that Spirit-led worship is out of control
    5. H.C.G. Moule: "We may be very sure that the command means nothing which shall 'unhinge' the Christian's life, and cast it loose from the noblest saint and the most steadfast order"
    6. Worship is free but not fanatical or fleshly
    7. Desire for God to have His way is evident
    8. Thanksgiving and praise are dominant
  B. THE SPIRIT-FILLED PERSON AND HIS WIFE OR HER HUSBAND (vv. 22–23)
    1. The Spirit-filled life is most evident in the home
    2. Moule: "The perfecting of the home is the masterpiece of the Gospel"
    3. Wives are submitted to their husbands as to the Lord

        a. The wife who is submitted to her husband is not a robot
        b. Neither must she discard all her natural abilities
        c. Her greatest joy, however, is in ministering to her husband
        d. His happiness is her delight and aim
    4. Husbands, love your wives even as Christ loved the church
        a. A sacrificial love . . . an enduring love
        b. An oft-repeated love . . . again and again
        c. His greatest joy is in ministering to his wife
        d. Her happiness is his delight and aim
    5. Two powerful principles that can revolutionize your home. What are they?
    6. These affect the entire family (6:1–4)
  C. THE SPIRIT-FILLED PERSON AND HIS WORK (6:5–9)
    1. The Spirit-filled workman does his work with all diligence
        a. He overcomes laziness and boredom
        b. He does his work as to the Lord, not to men
    2. The Spirit-filled employer treats employees as he would be treated
        a. Forbearing threatening
        b. Treat them as you want the Lord to treat you
    3. Let Christ be exalted in the workplace by employees and employers
III. CONCLUSION
  A. THE SPIRIT-FILLED LIFE IS ALL INCLUSIVE
  B. IN DAILY LIVING, THIS DEMANDS FULL SURRENDER

THANKSGIVING WITH PAUL

2 Corinthians 9:15; Romans 1:8–11; 1 Thessalonians 5:18

I. INTRODUCTION
  A. SOME GREAT PORTIONS ON THANKSGIVING IN THE BIBLE
    1. Exodus 15: Song of praise and thanksgiving
    2. Psalm 100: David's song of thanksgiving
  B. WE HAVE MUCH FOR WHICH TO THANK GOD
  C. THANKSGIVING WITH PAUL

II. BODY
  A. PAUL THANKFUL FOR CHRIST (2 Cor. 9:15; 1 Cor. 15:57)
    1. The two great things about salvation in Christ to Paul: The empty grave and the eternal gift
    2. The empty grave
      a. Paul's hatred of Christ before the cross
      b. Finally, Paul's friends had crucified Jesus to end it all
      c. Then, suddenly, He was there again: the resurrection!
      d. Paul guards the coats of those who stone Stephen
      e. Paul puts many to death
      f. The encounter with Christ on the Damascus road: "I am Jesus" (Acts 9:1–9)
      g. Then he knew that Christ was alive
    3. The eternal gift (2 Cor. 9:15)
      a. Paul had tried so hard before, had been so religious
      b. Found that salvation was a gift to receive (Eph. 2:8–9)
    4. Are you thankful today for your living Savior?
    5. Are you thankful for salvation?
  B. PAUL THANKFUL FOR CHRISTIANS (Phil. 1:3; Rom. 1:8–11)
    1. "Upon every remembrance of you"
    2. Paul had a great love for the saints (Rom. 1:8)
    3. Jesus: "If you have love one for the other" (John 13:35)
      a. Love longs for fellowship

   b. What brings you back to church?

   c. We ought to long to see the saints

  4. Sometimes Christians do not live up to their potential

   a. Sometimes they do not talk like Christians

   b. Sometimes they do not walk like Christians

  5. But there ought to be fierce loyalty among Christians

  6. Can you be thankful for those sitting around you?

  7. Are you thankful for all believers?

 C. PAUL THANKFUL CONSTANTLY (1 Thess. 5:18)

  1. "In everything give thanks."

   a. Stoned, shipwrecked, imprisoned: "Thank you, Lord"

   b. Poor eyesight, not handsome, short: "Thank you, Lord"

   c. Not enough gifts from the churches: "Thank you, Lord"

  2. The secret of thanksgiving for the Thessalonians

   a. The letter's theme is Christ's return

   b. Everyday, his Lord expected

III. CONCLUSION

 A. ARE YOU AS THANKFUL AS PAUL?

 B. IF NOT, WHY NOT?

 C. LET'S BE THANKFUL EVERY DAY AND SO HONOR OUR LORD

WITH CHRIST IN THANKSGIVING

I. INTRODUCTION
 A. THE PLANS FOR THANKSGIVING PRETTY WELL
    COMPLETED
    1. Thanksgiving dinner with the family
    2. Probably a day of food and football
 B. IF JESUS CAME TO YOUR HOUSE
    1. If you are a Christian, Christ will come to your house
    2. For what would Jesus give thanks?

II. BODY
 A. CHRIST THANKFUL FOR THE SIMPLICITY OF THE
    GOSPEL (Matt. 11:25)
    1. The scene: Christ's ministry (vv. 5, 6, 20–24)
       a. Christ and His outreach to the poor and needy
       b. Rejection by the proud cities and Pharisees
    2. The great mistake (1 Cor. 1:17, 18; Rom. 1:20–24)
    3. The road to blessing is the road of humility
       a. Humble yourself under the mighty hand of God
          (1 Peter 5:16)
       b. "He that humbleth himself shall be exalted" (Luke
          14:11)
    4. Christ thankful, as He looked over the multitude, that
       education, riches, and fame could not earn heaven
    5. You must come to Christ as a little child
 B. CHRIST THANKFUL FOR THE SUFFICIENCY OF THE
    FATHER (John 6:11)
    1. The setting and the scene: Feeding of the five thousand
    2. The need and the resources at hand
       a. How would you like to have that crowd drop in for
          Thanksgiving?
       b. Philip's dilemma: not enough to meet this need
       c. Jesus proving Philip . . . Philip would be a better
          man
       d. The comfort . . . He knew what He would do

      3. Christ thankful for the provision
        a. He made the universe, yet was thankful for loaves and fishes
        b. Called forth the first stalk of wheat, yet was thankful for bread
        c. Spoke the first fishes into existence, yet was thankful for those given to Him
      4. How little we show our thankfulness!
      5. How much we take for granted!

  C. CHRIST THANKFUL FOR SALVATION THROUGH THE CROSS (1 Cor. 11:23–24)
      1. Christ with the disciples in the Upper Room at time of the Passover
      2. Thanksgiving for the food
      3. But this is not just thanksgiving for the food
        a. "This is my body which is broken for you."
        b. "This is the New Testament in my blood."
      4. What amazing love! Thankful even for the cross
      5. Thankful that men can be saved even though it takes the cross

III. CONCLUSION
  A. HOW WILL YOUR THANKSGIVING MEASURE UP?
  B. WHAT ARE YOU GOING TO DO ABOUT IT?

BURDEN LIFTING DAY

I. INTRODUCTION
  A. GOD'S PROPHETIC PLAN IS ALWAYS ON SCHEDULE
    1. Some periods seem to witness a faster pace of fulfillment
    2. Examples of seemingly slow times
      a. Israel in captivity 400 years
      b. The 400 years of silence
    3. Examples of swift fulfillment
      a. The deliverance from Egypt
      b. The time of the birth of Christ
      c. This present time
  B. THE CURTAIN OPENS
    1. Preparation for the birth of Christ
    2. This preparation begins by the announcement of another birth, John
  C. ZACHARIAS AND ELISABETH
    1. Zacharias was a priest
    2. Elisabeth of the line of Aaron

II. BODY
  A. THE BURDEN IN THEIR LIVES (v. 7)
    1. They had no child
      a. Elisabeth was barren
      b. They were both now well stricken in years
    2. Only a few verses after we meet them, we're aware of this
      a. This must have been paramount in their thoughts
      b. Others knew this was their problem
      c. Could not know them long without this being known
    3. Good people . . . but
    4. Perhaps your burden eclipses all of your blessings
      a. You have come with it today
      b. What is your burden?

    (1) Is it a wrong relationship with others?
    (2) Is it ill health? Money trouble? Home trouble?
    (3) Is there some besetting sin?
  B. BURDEN-LIFTING DAY ARRIVED (vv. 8–11)
    1. Today the answer to their prayers would come
    2. Today the longing in each of them would be satisfied, the empty place filled
    3. Some things to notice about that day
      a. It was an ordinary day preceded by an ordinary yesterday
      b. They carried out their ordinary duties
      c. Zacharias went to the temple as usual
      d. It was a day of prayer
    4. Burden-lifting days in the Bible
      a. Blind Bartimaeus outside Jericho (Mark 10:46–52)
      b. Crooked Zacchaeus up the tree (Luke 19:1–10)
      c. The Samaritan woman at the well (John 4:1–42)
  C. WHEN THEIR BURDEN WAS LIFTED, THE BLESSINGS WERE FAR GREATER THAN THEY HAD EXPECTED (vv. 12–25 and 58–66)
    1. They had hoped for a baby
      a. One to whom they could show their love
      b. One in whom they could see themselves
      c. One who could keep their memory alive in the neighborhood
    2. God gave them a child still remembered . . . as they are
      a. Multitudes would come to hear him preach
      b. Even wicked Herod was in his congregation
    3. The forerunner of Christ
    4. The angel's announcement . . . the birth (vv. 19–25 and 58–66)
    5. The prophecy of Zacharias (Luke 1:67–80)
 III. CONCLUSION
  A. WHAT IS YOUR BURDEN? YOUR AREA OF DEFEAT? YOUR NEED?
  B. GOD WILL MEET YOUR NEED TODAY

FEAR NOT

I. INTRODUCTION
  A. TIMES WHEN GOD SEEMS SLOW
    1. Sometimes God seems to be moving at high speed
    2. At other times it seems that He is so slow in His program
      a. The four hundred years of silence between testaments
      b. Words of the prophets must have seemed vain
  B. THE WHIRLWIND PACE THEN AND NOW
    1. Angels sent on special errands
    2. John the Baptist to be born . . . other miracles
  C. SUDDENLY THOSE WHO HAD WAITED WERE GRIPPED WITH FEAR

II. BODY
  A. THE FEAR OF THE UNEXPECTED (Luke 1:26–30)
    1. "Fear not, Mary."
    2. Mary's life up to then very normal
      a. Growing up . . . dreaming romantic dreams like all girls
      b. Kept herself right with God
      c. She was engaged and anticipating marriage
    3. What is this that has entered her peaceful harbor to make waves? She was troubled at his saying
      a. Easy to panic at the unexpected
      b. The best made plans may go wrong
      c. Some fear all interruptions: Every phone call a threat, every letter opened fearfully
    4. But what good news the angel brought that day!
    5. She had found favor with God and would be part of a miracle
  B. THE FEAR OF PERSONAL LOSS (Matt. 1:18–25)
    1. Joseph and Mary . . . all he had dreamed about or hoped for
    2. Then the awful blow: Mary was with child

        a. Joseph's dreams are shattered.
        b. His castles tumble
        c. He thought he would lose Mary
        d. How real these fears are: Our children or other family members
    3. Note that Joseph was not afraid of the angel . . . but of loss
    4. We may fear personal loss
        a. Loss of money
        b. Loss of home
        c. Loss of name
    5. How this holds back blessing
        a. Afraid to risk love
        b. Afraid to risk investment
        c. Afraid to live
    6. Joseph would not lose Mary and would gain more than he had ever imagined
  C. THE FEAR OF MEETING GOD (Luke 2:8–14)
    1. The fearful shepherds
    2. Their fear was because of the glory of the Lord
    3. Many have shared that fear and awe
        a. Abraham, Job, Isaiah, Peter
        b. They must have faced their sins
    4. You may fear meeting God
    5. But here's good news: God loves you and sent His Son to be your Savior

III. CONCLUSION
  A. GOD WANTS TO TAKE AWAY YOUR FEARS
  B. TRUST HIM AND YOU WILL HAVE NOTHING TO FEAR

ON TIME AND ON TARGET

I. INTRODUCTION
    A. GIFT GIVING AT CHRISTMAS AND PREACHING
        1. Especially in America: "Buy me! Take me home!"
        2. Preaching at Christmas is like that
            a. Preach me: The inn, the shepherds, the wise men!
            b. The prophecies and the angelic appearances!
    B. TODAY . . . CHRISTMAS WITH PAUL
        1. His statement about Christ's birth to the Galatian church
        2. All his statement encompasses

II. BODY
    A. GOD IS ALWAYS ON TIME
        1. "When the fullness of the time was come."
        2. How impatient we become when things don't work out as planned: When our prayers are not answered or when difficulties persist
        3. But God is always on time!
        4. Consider some Old Testament examples:
            a. Joseph sold into slavery and imprisoned. He becomes the prime minister of Egypt
            b. Moses preserved in the desert becomes the deliverer
            c. The Red Sea experience: The sea opened just in time
        5. God was right on time with the birth of Christ
            a. How long it must have seemed!
            b. The promise in the Garden, the prophecies, the silence
            c. Then, ACTION: angelic activity
            d. The taxing, the crowded inn, the birth, the shepherds, the wise men
        6. God will be right on time with the Second Coming of Christ

        a.   The current scene and temptations to date setting
        b.   Some doubt, but God will be on time
    7.   God is always on time in His working in our lives
        a.   You are not here by accident
        b.   Your difficulties are opportunities to believe

B. GOD MEETS PEOPLE WHERE THEY ARE
    1. "God sent forth His Son, made of a woman, made under the law . . ."
    2. That's where we all had our beginning
        a.   Born so helpless
        b.   How strange that God should choose this entrance to the world
    3. How great the degree of His humility (Phil. 2:5–7)
    4. Laid in a manger
    5. God will meet you where you are today

C. GOD WANTS TO CHANGE PEOPLE FROM WHAT THEY ARE TO WHAT THEY CAN BE!!
    1. "That we might receive the adoption of sons"
    2. Adoption means "son placed"
    3. Adoption possible because of redemption . . . the cross
    4. God is developing you into what you ought to be

III. CONCLUSION

A. JESUS WILL CHANGE YOUR LIFE
B. YOU CAN ONLY BE WHAT YOU OUGHT TO BE THROUGH HIS POWER
C. MAKE THIS YOUR MOMENT OF DECISION: THE MOST IMPORTANT IN YOUR LIFE

THE APPEARANCE TO JOSEPH

I. INTRODUCTION
  A. ANGELIC APPEARANCES AND THE BIRTH OF CHRIST
    1. Four hundred years of silence
    2. Suddenly a flurry of prophetic action
      a. To Zacharias, to Mary, to Joseph
      b. The appearance to the shepherds
  B. THE OTHER PRINCIPAL CHARACTER IN THIS SACRED SCENE WELL KNOWN
    1. Must not leave out Joseph
    2. Must have seemed to him that this had been done

II. BODY
  A. THE MAN JOSEPH (vv. 18–20)
    1. He was of the house and lineage of David
      a. This will later take him and Mary to Bethlehem
      b. The Roman Empire gets involved in the miracle through its taxing
    2. He is evidently a poor man: the turtledoves at dedication (Luke 2:24)
    3. He falls in love with Mary and dreams of the future
    4. He is betrothed to Mary: engaged
      a. Betrothal then: Two witnesses, word pledged, money given
      b. Sacred as marriage: Violation was very serious
    5. Joseph's world comes crashing in!
      a. Mary is with child
      b. No simple solution
    6. Joseph a just and merciful man so decides to put her away privily
  B. THE MESSAGE TO JOSEPH (vv. 20–21)
    1. "While he thought on these things."
      a. Couldn't think on anything else
      b. Maybe something is preying on your mind
    2. God had a message for Joseph in this hour of his trouble

      3. A personal message: "Joseph, thou son of David."
      4. "Fear not!" Those good words again
      5. That which is conceived in her is of the Holy Ghost
         a. Seemed the furthest from Joseph's expectations
         b. Seemed sinful . . . now sacred . . . sanctified
         c. Seemed sure to bring death . . . now deliverance
         d. Seemed sure to ruin Mary's good name . . . now will immortalize it
         e. Seemed that all would call her bad . . . instead she would be called blessed
      6. Thought it the end of his dreams as a husband . . . found it to be the answer to his dreams as a man

  C. THE MIRACULOUS BIRTH OF CHRIST (vv. 21–25)
      1. The birth of the Savior was to save His people from their sins
      2. Fulfilling the prophecies of the Old Testament
      3. Matthew explains Isaiah 7:14
      4. The absolute necessity of the Virgin Birth of Christ
      5. This miraculous birth makes possible the new birth

III. CONCLUSION
  A. THE APPLICATION OF THE ANGEL'S MESSAGE
  B. GOD WILL MEET YOU IN YOUR DESPAIR
  C. THE GOOD NEWS OF THE SAVIOR'S BIRTH IS FOR YOU

THE NAME JESUS

I. INTRODUCTION
   A. THE TIME ARRIVES AT LAST
   B. THE SETTING AND THE SCENE
      1. The glad moments of Joseph's love for Mary
      2. Joseph's world tumbles . . . Mary is with child
      3. The angel's message: "Fear not." The giving of the name
   C. THE NAME JESUS

II. BODY
   A. THE ORIGIN OF THE NAME (Matt. 1:21)
      1. Moses seems to have originated the name
         a. Numbers 13:8–16 . . . *Oshea* means "salvation."
         b. Jehovah and Oshea . . . God's salvation (v. 16)
         c. "Joshua" in the Old Testament same as "Jesus" in the New Testament
      2. Joshua as a type or picture of Jesus
         a. Born in slavery then exalted to be ruler of his people
         b. Followed the rule of Moses . . . law to grace (John 1:17)
         c. Led the wandering people from the wilderness to Canaan
         d. Led successfully over Jordan
         e. Walls fell before him (Eph. 2:14)
         f. Led his people to victory
   B. THE IMPACT OF THE NAME "JESUS" BECAUSE IT WAS GIVEN TO CHRIST
      1. Really quite a common name in that day
      2. Many had copied the name of the great leader of Israel, Joshua
      3. Christ made the common uncommon
         a. From the time that the babe was called "Jesus" it was not common

      b. That name meant salvation to the shepherds
      c. That name meant healing to the helpless
      d. That name meant destruction to the demons
      e. That name meant life to the lepers
      f. That name meant resurrection to the dead
   4. The name that brings salvation today (Acts 4:12)
      a. The danger of Christmas: Settling for traditions
      b. Get past the tinsel to the Truth
   5. What does the name Jesus mean to you today?

C. THE IMPORTANCE OF THE NAME JESUS IN THE FUTURE
   1. The name Jesus is associated with the coming resurrection (1 Thess. 4:13)
   2. The name Jesus and the judgment (Phil. 2:10)
   3. The name Jesus and future events (Rev. 1:1; 22:16)
   4. The name that will help you today

III. CONCLUSION
A. WHY THE BABE WAS TO BE CALLED JESUS
   1. He would save His people from their sins
   2. Joseph must have been overwhelmed
   3. Cleansing for Joseph and us
B. HE WILL SAVE YOU FROM YOUR SINS

GOOD NEWS FOR SHEPHERDS
AND OTHER SINNERS

SERIES ON THE BIRTH OF CHRIST   *Luke* 2:10–11

I. INTRODUCTION
  A. THE BIRTH IN BETHLEHEM
    1. How long the world had waited!
    2. But finally the hour arrived
      a. The angelic messages
      b. The taxing
      c. The journey to Bethlehem
    3. The birth in the stable . . . no spotless hospital
      a. The sounds and smells of the stable
      b. No doctor . . . but a doctor chosen to tell the story
  B. ANNOUNCING THE NEWS TO THE SHEPHERDS
    1. The first to know were humble shepherds
    2. How fitting that the Lamb of God was born in a manger!

II. BODY
  A. THE END OF FEAR (v. 10)
    1. "Fear not." Those two good words always in the vocabulary of angels
    2. The shepherds were afraid, but this runs deeper
      a. The first evidence of the fall was fear (Gen. 3:8–10)
      b. Fear stalking men through the centuries since
        (1) Abraham lying about Sarah because of fear (Gen. 12:11–13)
        (2) Jacob afraid of Esau (Gen. 32:6–8)
        (3) Moses afraid of Pharoah and of rejection (Exod. 4:1)
        (4) Israel afraid to enter the Promised Land (Num. 14)
    3. Jesus would move through the area He traveled dispelling fear
      a. The disciples and the storm
      b. Blind Bartimaeus feared he would never see
      c. Ten lepers feared they would never be with their families

        d. Mary and Martha feared they would never see Lazarus again
    4. Fears at Christmas:
        a. Health
        b. Family
        c. World conditions
        d. Economy
        e. Life
    5. Faith the opposite of fear: saved by faith and kept by faith
  B. THE BIRTH OF JOY (v. 10)
    1. "Good tidings of great joy."
    2. The songs of Christmas about joy
    3. Why this joy?
        a. Because the Savior has been born
        b. Because the Scripture has been fulfilled
        c. Because Christ is Lord
    4. Come to Him and have joy. Trust Him
  C. THE BEGINNING OF EVANGELISM (v. 10)
    1. "Which shall be to all people."
    2. All need this Savior
        a. All are sinners (Rom. 3:23)
        b. Christ died for all (Rom. 5:8)
    3. He is available to all people
    4. The actions of the shepherds
        a. We also are to be going with the good news
        b. Not to sit and soak on the way to heaven

III. CONCLUSION
  A. GOD MEETS US WHERE WE ARE
  B. COME TO JESUS WITH YOUR SINS AND FEARS AND BE SAVED
  C. TELL THE GOOD NEWS TO ALL!

THE LAST INVITATION IN THE BIBLE

Revelation 22:17

I. INTRODUCTION
   A. THE INVITATION AT THE CLOSE OF THE SERVICE
      1. The call for sinners to be saved, backsliders reclaimed
      2. The call to those with special needs and burdens
      3. After the preaching comes the invitation
   B. THE LAST INVITATION IN THE BIBLE
      1. After all the prophecy, one final invitation
      2. Many invitations in the Bible
         a. Genesis 7:1, "Come thou and all thine house into the ark"
         b. Nearly 2,000 times our Lord invites people to come to Him
      3. The last call

II. BODY
   A. GOD'S GREATEST BURDEN
      1. The Spirit says, "Come"
      2. The Holy Spirit invites people to salvation today
         a. He convicts of sin
         b. He enters the heart when the sinner calls
         c. He abides all through life, comforting, convicting, empowering
      3. The work of inviting people is God's greatest burden
         a. Greater than creation or maintaining creation
         b. Greater than moving the nations in prophecy's pattern
         c. Greater than keeping the planets in their courses
      4. God's burden because of His love
   B. THE CHURCH'S GREATEST BUSINESS
      1. " . . . and the bride say come"
      2. The bride is the church, and the church is to be inviting
      3. This is the greatest responsibility of the church
      4. How busy we get with other things to the devil's delight!

        a. The performing of religious ceremonies or forms
        b. The holding of conferences and the pushing of projects
        c. The business of the church, money, etc
    5. But our most important function is to invite people to Christ
    6. "Let him that heareth" . . . even the new converts are to be involved

C. MANKIND'S GREATEST BLESSING
    1. "And let him that is athirst come"
    2. How thirsty the world is!
        a. The woman at the well
        b. Coming to the Lord quenches one's thirst
    3. The requirement for coming: One must be thirsty
        a. Any age may come, any race may come
        b. Anyone may come regardless of past sins
        c. Anyone may come regardless of social or financial position
    4. Do you feel thirsty? Come!

D. LIFE'S GREATEST BARGAIN
    1. "Take of the water of life freely"
    2. The price has been paid: the blood of Christ
    3. Free water for thirsty souls
    4. Come and drink and be satisfied (Isa. 55:1)

III. CONCLUSION
    A. THE CALL TO THOSE WHO NEED TO COME AND DRINK OF LIVING WATER
    B. THE CALL TO THOSE WHO NEED TO GET INVOLVED IN SHARING THE INVITATION

DON'T LOOK BACK!

Luke 9:62

I. INTRODUCTION
   A. SATCHEL PAIGE AND HIS GOOD RULE FOR LIVING
      1. "Don't look back, something may be gaining on you"
      2. The Bible also calls for not looking back
   B. LOOKING BACK HINDERS FORWARD PROGRESS
      1. Looking back may be making you depressed
      2. Looking back may be bringing you defeat

II. BODY
   A. DON'T LOOK BACK AT SINS THAT HAVE BEEN FOR-GIVEN
      1. I John 1:7–9 guarantees forgiveness of all sins
      2. God really does put our sins away (Psalm 103)
      3. Perhaps you believe this for others, but not for yourself
      4. But God has put away all sin, even your most serious ones
   B. DON'T LOOK BACK AT DEFEATS THAT GET YOU DOWN
      1. All people have some defeats in their past
      2. Only those who never attempt anything are free from failing
      3. But see Psalm 37:23–24, God lifts up those who fall
      4. Don't allow failing to make you feel you are a failure
   C. DON'T LOOK BACK AT THE PAST AND SEE IT BETTER THAN IT WAS (Eccl. 7:10)
      1. Israel looking back to Egypt (Num. 11:18)
      2. Distance lends enchantment
      3. Nostalgia is never quite honest
      4. Vance Havner: "The present is never as good as it used to be"
      5. A great future beats a great past every time
   D. DON'T LOOK BACK AT OLD CONFLICTS THAT MAKE YOU BITTER
      1. If you rehearse old conflicts the hurt returns
      2. Rehashing these opens old wounds

3. Even those where forgiveness has taken place will become dangerous again if you keep going over them
4. Forget the past and get on with profitable living (1 Peter 2:1–2)

E. DON'T LOOK BACK AT OLD VICTORIES THAT MAY CAUSE YOU TO THINK YOU HAVE ARRIVED (Phil. 3:13–14)
1. Here is the primary message of Philippians 3:13–14
2. I served the Lord with all my heart . . . once
3. I was a soul winner . . . once
4. I was sold out to Christ . . . once
5. What about today?

III. CONCLUSION

A. LOOK UP! LOOKING UNTO JESUS (Heb. 12:1–2)
B. LOOK ON THE FIELDS AND IN CARING FOR OTHERS YOU WILL FORGET THE PAST
C. LOOK AHEAD! THE BEST IS YET TO COME!

ALL ABOUT CHRISTIAN GIVING

2 Corinthians 9

I. INTRODUCTION
  A. GIVING: A MISUNDERSTOOD AND MISUSED PART OF THE CHRISTIAN LIFE
    1. Those who make money raising everything
    2. Those who use gimmicks
    3. Those who make giving an unimportant part of the Christian life
  B. THE BIBLE LAYS DOWN PRINCIPLES FOR GIVING

II. BODY
  A. WE CAN NEVER ENRICH GOD WITH OUR GIVING (1 Chron. 29:9–14)
    1. David, near death, prepares the people to build the temple
    2. The tremendous offering (vv. 5–9)
    3. But even all this cannot enrich God
      a. He owns the cattle on a thousand hills
      b. All that is in heaven and earth belongs to Him
    4. No wonder a man cannot buy his way into heaven
    5. No wonder you cannot gain favor with God by your giving
    6. God wants your heart, then your offerings
  B. WE SHOULD GIVE REGULARLY AND SYSTEMATICALLY
    1. "Upon the first day of the week" (1 Cor. 16:1–2)
    2. Some give great sums spasmodically
      a. This may seem more impressive
      b. Some give only when moved by some great need
    3. Some intend to leave a great amount when they die
    4. The Bible teaches a weekly accounting of our giving
    5. Systematically: "As God hath prospered him"
      a. No "tipping" please
      b. A percentage of what God has given
    6. Old Testament examples of percentage giving
      a. Abraham gave tithes of all he possessed (Gen. 14:20)

205

      b. Jacob: "Of all that thou shalt give me I will surely give the tenth to thee" (Gen. 28:22)

      c. Malachi 3:10, "Bring ye all the tithes into the storehouse"

    7. This percentage should come off the top: the firstfruits

    8. Under grace our giving should exceed that under law

C. WE SHOULD GIVE GENEROUSLY AND CHEERFULLY, EXPECTING THAT GOD WILL MEET OUR NEEDS (2 Cor. 9:6–9)

    1. "Not grudgingly or of necessity"

      a. Do not give if you do not want to give

      b. Do not give more than you can give cheerfully

    2. The context of Philippians 4:19

    3. The expectation of giving:

      a. "He which soweth sparingly shall reap also sparingly" (v. 6)

      b. Giving your way to prosperity

III. CONCLUSION

    A. HOW DOES YOUR GIVING MEASURE UP?

    B. ARE YOU WILLING TO TAKE GOD INTO THIS PART OF YOUR LIFE?

    C. ADVENTURES IN GIVING

PROTECTION IN STORMS

Acts 27; 28:1-6

I. INTRODUCTION
  A. PAUL'S DESIRE TO GO TO HOME
     1. He was going now as a prisoner
     2. Even so, he would have great success there
        a. Members of Caesar's household would be converted
        b. His experience in Rome is condensed in Acts 28:30-31
  B. OUR TEXT GIVES THE STORY OF GOD'S PROTECTION OF PAUL ON THE JOURNEY
II. BODY
  A. PROTECTION IN THE STORM (27:14-41)
     1. This shows God's protection from natural storms
     2. The great storm called *euroclydon* (v. 14)
     3. The crew struggles to keep the ship afloat (vv. 16-20)
        a. Lightening the ship
        b. Even the prisoners help work for survival
     4. Paul cared for during the storm
        a. He was the only one with a word from the Lord (vv. 22-24)
        b. His word from the Lord placed him in command of the situation (vv. 30-33)
     5. Our Lord has also promised to be with us in the storms of life
  B. PROTECTION FROM THE SOLDIERS (v. 42)
     1. This shows God's protection from national storms
     2. Their purpose was to kill all the prisoners
     3. Christians have suffered much at the hands of nations
        a. Persecution of the early church by Rome
        b. Persecutions under Hitler and leaders of Communism
     4. Actually, all aboard saved for Paul's sake
        a. God has often spared or blessed many for the sake

of a few faithful ones (Gen. 18:27–33; 26:24; 39:5;
1 Kings 11:11–13; 2 Kings 8:19)

    b. America may be spared because of a few righteous
people

  5. How important are you to your country?

C. PROTECTION FROM THE SERPENT (28:1–6)

  1. This shows God's protection from supernatural storms

  2. The serpent a symbol of the devil

  3. This one came out of the fire and attached itself to Paul

  4. The reaction of the natives:

    a. First they thought he would die

    b. Later they worshiped him as a god

  5. As believers, we are guaranteed God's protection from
the serpent

    a. Limits on the tempter (1 Cor. 10:13)

    b. The One in us is greater (1 John 4:4)

III. CONCLUSION

A. NO PLACE AS SAFE AS IN THE PERFECT WILL OF GOD

  1. We are protected until our work is done

  2. After the course is run, heaven awaits

  3. We are winners either way

B. SURRENDER THEN TO THE LORD AND LET HIM HAVE
HIS WAY WITH YOUR LIFE

  1. You will benefit in earthly fellowship and protection

  2. Your rewards will endure forever

MEET MY GOOD SAMARITAN

Luke 10:25–37

I. INTRODUCTION
   A. THE LAWYER AND HIS QUESTION
      1. It was a good question
      2. The Lord's challenging answer (v. 27)
      3. The lawyer seeks an escape (v. 29)
   B. THE USUAL INTERPRETATION OF THE PARABLE OF THE GOOD SAMARITAN
      1. To teach responsibility to our neighbor
      2. To show who is our neighbor
   C. ANOTHER APPLICATION OF THIS FAMILIAR PARABLE

II. BODY
   A. LET THE CERTAIN MAN REPRESENT ANY SINNER (v. 30)
      1. From Jerusalem to Jericho
         a. Jerusalem is the city of peace
         b. Jericho is the city of the curse
         c. The road from Jerusalem to Jericho is downward
      2. He fell among thieves
         a. Satan is a thief (John 10:10)
         b. The thief in Eden and here today
      3. The thieves left him stripped and half dead
         a. Stripped . . . without righteousness
         b. Half dead . . . all are dead spiritually (Eph. 2:1–9)
   B. LET THE PRIEST AND THE LEVITE REPRESENT ALL EMPTY SOLUTIONS FOR SINNERS
      1. The priest represents the condemnation of the law
         a. "You should not have come this way"
         b. At best, the law can but condemn
      2. The Levite represents religious instruction and ceremony
         a. "I can tell you the route you should have taken"
         b. "I can tell you the route to take next time"
         c. Neither of these meets the poor, naked, half-dead traveler in his need

      3. The human heart is in need of more than exposition and instruction
      4. Lost people need salvation
  C. LET THE GOOD SAMARITAN REPRESENT THE SAVIOR FOR SINNERS
      1. The Samaritan was a rejected person (Isa. 53:3)
      2. As he journeyed (he had a definite destination)
      3. He came where he was (Luke 19:10; Phil. 2:5–8)
      4. He had compassion on him (our Lord's compassion)
      5. He bound up his wounds . . . getting right to the heart of the problem
      6. He poured in wine (a disinfectant)
      7. He poured in oil (a symbol of the Holy Spirit)
      8. His care for the man afterward (v. 34)
      9. The injured man's care paid for until the Samaritan returned (v. 35)

III. CONCLUSION
  A. THE STORY STILL NOT FINISHED
  B. MEET MY GOOD SAMARITAN

TO WHOM SHALL WE GO?

John 6:68

I. INTRODUCTION
   A. THE MULTITUDES AND THE MASTER
      1. Familiar to speak of multitudes following Christ
      2. The great crowds, the feeding of the five thousand, etc.
   B. THE MULTITUDES TURNING AWAY, AS THEY DO TODAY
      1. The unpopular message: God's Son, the cross, His death
      2. The question of Jesus as the crowd leaves: "Will ye also go away?"
      3. Peter's question

II. BODY
   A. WE ALL NEED SOMEONE TO WHOM WE CAN GO (v. 68)
      1. God has not made man to be alone. Consider creation
      2. When he is sad, he needs someone to share his sorrows
      3. When he is glad, he needs someone to share his joy
      4. The value of God's plan for the home: husbands, wives and children
         a. Remember family times
         b. Memories of a mother or father
         c. Families gather in times of crisis
      5. The value of human friendships
   B. WE ALL NEED SOMEONE TO WHOM WE CAN GO WITH A WORD FROM ETERNITY (v. 68)
      1. "Thou hast the words of eternal life"
      2. Friends and family are important, but we come to times in life when we are beyond the power of earthly friends to help
      3. The wound may be so deep that we need a word from eternity
      4. At death, we see the shortness of life
         a. Threescore and ten . . . sometimes less . . . or more (Ps. 90:10)

           b. So tied to time: Moments, months, years
- 5. What about eternity?
- 6. Jesus knows all about eternity
  - a. He is the eternal one
  - b. He spoke of eternity, everlasting life and eternal life
- C. WE MAY ALL COME TO JESUS AND FIND HIM A FRIEND WHO HAS ALL THE ANSWERS FOR TIME AND ETERNITY
  1. "We believe and are sure that thou art that Christ, the Son of the living God" (John 6:69)
  2. How good to be sure!
  3. The calls of Christ to come to Him
     - a. "Him that cometh to me I will in no wise cast out" (John 6:37)
     - b. "Come unto me all ye that labor and are heavy laden" (Matt. 11:28)
     - c. "And the Spirit and the bride say come" (Rev. 22:17)
  4. What it means to come to Him in faith

III. CONCLUSION
  - A. COME THEN TO JESUS AND FIND HIM ALL YOU NEED
  - B. HE WILL PREPARE YOU FOR TIME AND ETERNITY

FOR SUCH A TIME AS THIS

Esther 4:10–17

I. INTRODUCTION
  A. THE SETTING AND THE SCENE
    1. The setting is Persia . . . Iran
    2. A time of great peril for the Jewish people
  B. FOUR PRINCIPLE CHARACTERS IN THE BOOK
    1. Ahasuerus, the powerful Persian king
    2. Esther, who becomes his queen
    3. Mordecai, Esther's kinsman
    4. Haman, the Jew hater. A forerunner of Hitler; he hated the Jews
  C. HAMAN'S PLAN: ESTHER CALLED UPON TO DELIVER HER PEOPLE

II. BODY
  A. ON THE DARKEST DAY, GOD MAKES A WAY (v. 14)
    1. Those were dark days for the Jews
    2. There have been many dark days for the Jews since
    3. We are living in dark days
      a. Communism on the march
      b. The moral decay of the past two decades
      c. The nuclear age and its prospects
    4. You may be passing through dark days now
      a. Dark days in your home, in your marriage, with your children
      b. Dark days in your business or on your job
      c. Dark days with your health, fears
      d. Dark days emotionally, no peace, tears near the surface
    5. BUT GOD DELIGHTS TO WORK IN THE DARK
      a. Creation's pattern . . . "Let there be light"
      b. Salvation's pattern . . . must realize we are lost
      c. Many Bible promises to those who are in trouble
    6. Mordecai's confidence . . . his optimistic faith
      a. The world needs to see it

      b. Look up
  B. GOD USES A WOMAN OR A MAN TO FULFILL HIS PLAN (v. 14)
    1. "... who knoweth whether thou art come to the kingdom . . . ?"
    2. God always has His person of the hour
      a. The mother of Moses in the time of darkness
      b. Moses, Gideon, David, others
      c. Luther, Wesley, Knox
      d. Spurgeon, Moody, Lanphier
    3. Perhaps you are God's person of the hour for America
    4. Perhaps you are God's person of the hour for this church
  C. ESTHER'S CRY WAS TO DO OR DIE (v. 16)
    1. "... if I perish, I perish"
    2. She is now willing to get involved
    3. She is now willing to lay all on the altar
    4. She is now willing to surrender all, to do her part
    5. She will be God's person to spare her people
    6. She concludes that quality of life is more important than duration

III. CONCLUSION
  A. THE CALL TO FULL SURRENDER
  B. THE CALL TO REAL INVOLVEMENT
  C. THE CALL TO OUTREACH

THANK GOD FOR YOU

Philippians 1:3

I. INTRODUCTION
   A. PAUL'S TENDER RELATIONSHIP WITH THE CHRISTIANS AT PHILIPPI
      1. He thanked God every time he thought of them
      2. We could use that kind of love today
   B. WRONG RELATIONSHIPS FLOURISH IN MANY CHURCHES TODAY
      1. People who cannot forgive
      2. Little groups gather and grumble
      3. The church becomes powerless because of lack of love
   C. LESSONS FROM PAUL'S STATEMENT OF THANKSGIVING

II. BODY
   A. THERE IS A VALUE IN REMEMBERING (v. 3)
      1. God has made us with the ability to remember
      2. Instructions to remember in the Bible
         a. "Remember now thy Creator" (Eccl. 12:1)
         b. "Remember Lot's wife" (Luke 17:32)
         c. "This do in remembrance of me" (1 Cor. 11)
         d. "Remember from whence thou art fallen" (Rev. 2:5)
      3. Paul remembers Philippi
         a. A little group by a river and Lydia's conversion
         b. The Philippian jailor
      4. Remember high points in your Christian life
         a. The day of your conversion
         b. The time you fully surrendered to the Lord
         c. Was there ever a better day?
   B. THERE IS A VALUE IN REMEMBERING POSITIVE THINGS ABOUT OTHERS
      1. "Every remembrance of you"
      2. Was the church at Philippi perfect?
         a. No perfect churches

215

   b. No perfect pastors
  3. Paul refused to dwell on the negatives about these people
   a. Were there gossips there? PROBABLY!
   b. Were there troublemakers there? PROBABLY!
   c. But Paul did not focus on these negative characteristics
  4. Paul thought about those who were faithful
   a. Some cared and shared
   b. Some gave sacrificially
   c. Some witnessed fervently
   d. Paul remembered these
  5. What do you think about when you think of this church?
  6. Are you thankful for some?
 C. THE VALUE OF EXPRESSING APPRECIATION TO THOSE WE LOVE
  1. Paul wasn't just thankful, he told them so
  2. What good is appreciation if it is never expressed?
  3. Like love, appreciation must be spoken . . . expressed!
  4. Letters to be written, calls to be made, people to see

III. CONCLUSION
 A. REMEMBERING TOGETHER
 B. FOR WHOM ARE YOU THANKFUL?
 C. THANK GOD FOR YOU!

THE CHRISTIAN HOME

Ephesians 5:18–32

I. INTRODUCTION
   A. THE HOME, THE MOST IMPORTANT UNIT OF LIFE
      1. It is the first unit ordained by God
      2. A nation is made up of homes
      3. The spiritual climate of a church is determined by its homes
   B. SO MANY TROUBLED HOMES TODAY
      1. That is why we have a troubled nation
      2. A greater threat than communism
   C. THE THRILLING CONTRAST
      1. A place where there is:
         a. Dedication instead of divorce
         b. Faith instead of fighting
         c. Harmony instead of hatred
         d. The Bible instead of a battle
      2. What is a Christian home?

II. BODY
   A. A CHRISTIAN HOME IS A PLACE WHERE THE LORD REIGNS
      1. The need of knowing Jesus Christ
      2. You cannot have a Christian home without Christ
         a. You can have a religious home
         b. You may even have a well-ordered home
      3. What a difference Christ makes!
      4. Not a formula but a faithful friend
      5. This is evidence of fullness of the Holy Spirit (Eph. 5:22–32)
      6. Christ, the unseen head of this home
   B. A CHRISTIAN HOME IS A PLACE WHERE LOVE REIGNS
      1. The wonderful, two-way love arrangement
         a. Wife lovingly submissive to her husband
         b. Husband loves and is not bitter toward his wife

    2. Some Christians have homes that are just the opposite of that
      a. Sort of an endurance contest
      b. Where they both put up with one another
    3. The one example God has chosen to demonstrate his walk with us
    4. The kind of love:
      a. That is deep in the heart
      b. Love that is sacrificial
      c. Love that is often expressed
    5. Read 1 Corinthians 13 again

  C. A CHRISTIAN HOME IS A PLACE WHERE THE BIBLE REIGNS
    1. The Bible is the Lord's way of cleansing (Ps. 119:9–11)
    2. Can't have a clean home without the Bible (Eph. 5:26–27)
    3. Attendance at church services should be a family affair
    4. God's instruction to Moses (Deut. 6:1–4)
    5. Your respect for the Bible measures your respect for God

III. CONCLUSION
  A. THE CALL TO DEDICATION IN HOME LIFE
  B. THE FAMILY ALTAR WILL ALTER YOUR HOME
  C. LET'S BUILD STRONG HOMES GOD'S WAY

THE MOST LOVED TEXT ON HEAVEN

John 14:1–6

I. INTRODUCTION
   A. THE FAMILIAR TEXT
      1. Good reasons for becoming so familiar
      2. Speaks a vital message to our hearts
   B. THE IMPORTANCE OF THIS TEST TO HURTING PEOPLE
      1. Because of its setting: Jesus soon to leave the disciples
      2. Because of its tenderness: A text overflowing with love

II. BODY
   A. THE ASSURANCE IN THIS TEXT (John 14:1)
      1. "Let not your heart be troubled"
      2. So many troubled people: fear, worry, doubts, dread of the future
      3. Notice how God seeks to relieve troubled hearts
         a. 1 Peter 5:7; Matthew 11:28–30; John 14:27
         b. The 365 "fear nots" of the Bible
      4. The twofold application of assurance
         a. For the person who has Christ as Savior at death
         b. For those who are left
      5. God to keep and guide them after Jesus was put to death
      6. Death could not end their fellowship
   B. THE ANTICIPATION IN THIS TEXT (vv. 2, 3)
      1. "In my Father's house there are many mansions"
      2. The anticipation of every Christian is threefold
      3. The anticipation of heaven. "I go to prepare a place for you"
         a. Death as departing (John 13:1; John 16:7; 2 Tim. 4:6)
         b. Indicates going from one place to another, the better place (Phil. 1:21; 2 Cor. 5:8)
      4. The anticipation of meeting Christ: "That where I am . . ."
         a. Would you like to meet the president?

219

            b. It will be better to meet Jesus
       5. The anticipation of meeting loved ones who have gone
           on before
   C. THE ANSWER IN THIS TEXT (vv. 5, 6)
       1. Thomas listening to these wonderful words wanted an
           answer
       2. How can we know the way?
       3. Jesus said, "I am the way"
           a. His death to pay for our sins
           b. His resurrection: He lives to save
       4. Note that Jesus is the *only* way

III. CONCLUSION
   A. CHRIST IS YOUR ANSWER
       1. He will bring assurance and peace to your heart
       2. He will give hope beyond the grave
   B. TRUST HIM AND SOLVE LIFE'S GREATEST PROBLEMS
       1. Guilt and fear will be gone
       2. Eternal life will be yours

SCRIPTURE INDEX